Löbëla

Löbëla

Justo Bolekia Boleká

TRANSLATED BY
Michael Ugarte

RESOURCE *Publications* · Eugene, Oregon

LÖBËLA

Copyright © 2015 Justo Bolekia Boleká. All rights reserved. Except for brief quotations in critical publications or reviews, no part of this book may be reproduced in any manner without prior written permission from the publisher. Write: Permissions. Wipf and Stock Publishers, 199 W. 8th Ave., Suite 3, Eugene, OR 97401.

Resource Publications
An Imprint of Wipf and Stock Publishers
199 W. 8th Ave., Suite 3
Eugene, OR 97401

www.wipfandstock.com

ISBN 13: 978-1-4982-0372-2

Manufactured in the U.S.A. 01/27/2015

To Judith Morgades, the first one to read my verses in 1978, later becoming my spouse and the mother of my children, Yeté and Ityökó.

To all those men and women who voluntarily or involuntarily figured out how to encourage me in this semiotic enterprise, people whose names I omit voluntarily.

To the reader (woman or man) whose life and images might manifest themselves in these verses, or the life and images of people known and unknown . . .

To you, *Löbëla*, incarnation of a woman whose life I search for in the caves and huts among the cries and dances, among the secrets and fortune.

Table of Contents

Introduction | ix

Muffled Cries / Gritos plegados | 1 / 1
The Elder Böekka / El anciano Böekka | 2 / 3
Servants Possessed / Siervos poseídos | 4 / 5
Braided Life / Vida trenzada | 6 / 7
Ancestral Times / Tiempos de antaño | 8 / 9
The Last Lance / La última lanza | 10 / 11
Afternoon Psalm / El salmo del atardecer | 12 / 14
Before You / Antes que tú | 16 / 17
Ö Má Löe (The Goodbye) / Ö má löe (El Adios) | 18 / 19
Misty Waters / Aguas en bruma | 20 / 21
The Ancestral Dance / El baile ancestral | 22 / 23
The Last Damsel / La última doncella | 24 / 26
The Boatman's Song / El canto del barquero | 28 / 29
The Beauty of All Time / La Bella de los Tiempos | 30 / 31
Image and Blood / Imagen y sangre | 32 / 33
Pool of Tears / Charca lacrimal | 34 / 35
The Goddess Löbëla / La ondina Löbëla | 36 / 37
Dust and Moon / Polvo y luna | 38 / 39
The Versed Path / El camino en verso | 40 / 41
Song / El canto | 42 / 43
Wésëpa! / ¡Wésëpa! | 44 / 46
Hollows and Hills / Hoyos y montes | 48 / 49
Versed Secrets / Secretos versados | 50 / 51
Löbëla / Löbëla | 52 / 54
The Ballad of Löbëla / La balada de Löbëla | 56 / 58

Table of Contents

Löbëla and Úri / Löbëla y Úri | 60 / 62
Hidden Heat / La oculta candencia | 64 / 65
Cries and Laughter / Llantos y risas | 66 / 67
Distant Loneliness / Soledad lejana | 68 / 69
Amalia's Secret / El secreto de Amalia | 70 / 72
Woman of the Valley / La mujer del valle | 74 / 76
Muted Cries / Gritos enmudecidos | 78 / 79
Furtive Verses / Versos furtivos | 80 / 81
Memories / Recuerdos | 82 / 83
Snail and Snake / Caracol y serpiente | 84 / 85
Sudden Desire / Presto deseo | 86 / 87
Voices / Voces | 88 / 89
Rátyííla la Bö (Twenty and Ten) / Rátyííla la bö (Veinte y diez) | 90 / 91
Furtive Lover / Amante furtivo | 92 / 93
Dancing and Shouting / Gritos y danzas | 94 / 95
Wrinkled Rocks / Rocas arcilladas | 96 / 97
Furtive Tears / Lágrimas furtivas | 98 / 99
Echo and Chaos / Eco y caos | 100 / 101
Waters and Moon / Aguas y Luna | 102 / 103
Eyes and Logs / Ojos y leños | 104 / 105
The Final Step / El paso final | 106 / 107
The Sentence / La sentencia | 108 / 109
The Date / La cita | 110 / 111

Epilogue / Epílogo | 112 / 113

The Damsels of Old / Las doncellas de antaño | 114 / 115
A Look Inside / Mirada adentro | 116 / 117
Sunken Eyes / Ojos hundidos | 118 / 119
Love? / ¿Amor? | 120 / 120

Thoughts from the Translator | 121

Introduction

And since it must be said, I should say it. I have never aimed to express myself in verse, perhaps because in poetry there is a collection of symbols not everyone will understand, and the song that goes with those verses is unheard, thus a common reader will probably not be able to digest the information contained in them through a conventional written code. I hope that my verses will contribute to a better assimilation of the message I want to convey; images that reveal an internalization of my specific condition as a man culturally and anthropologically defined within a specific place.

With the title *Löbëla* I offer poems divided in three parts. In the first I compile and deform the cultural dimensions of my life that served (and still do) as referents for me. I engage in this deformation to facilitate a comprehension of all that remains and was "my" ancestral Bubi culture. In the second part, through an imaginary, yet by no means unreal, Löbëla, I narrate the sobbing and crying that come from the confusion between reality and desire, always trying to remain loyal to those "Versed Secrets"; I want to describe a limbo broken, stripped, no longer whole–a process I have called "transformation," individual or collective, psychological or cultural. The third part, "Furtive Verses," is the synthesis of the two previous, a synthesis of an ancient yesterday and a recent yesterday where the present serves as a vehicle to fuse the two. In this synthesis the inherent facts (the tangible reality) is of utmost importance; we can never separate them from the world of the narrator and his companion. All in all, there is a substantial dose of fiction in these verses, fantasy as well as an expression of the individual's desire to transform one's surroundings, the previous internalization of everything we observe, desire, abhor, reject, destroy, and long for, an intention of being and seeing oneself as a manifestation of nature.

It is not easy to articulate all one's desires in so few verses. Much less knowing they are specifically directed to a Bubi reader, and at the same time transformed into a sign system that doesn't belong to that specific reader. It is possible that the reader might adapt what he assimilates from his reading, or decoding, to his social milieu, always considering his own experience. But let's remember that it is not my intention to recreate a static world, a world anchored in times gone by in order to justify a collective stasis or

Introduction

retrogression. One should not extrapolate this experience, individual or collective, to aspects of life not integrally connected to the history of each individual. Every experience of every individual manifests a world view.

The individual, as an agent of history and a transformer of reality, should search independently for the reason he was created. This is somewhat difficult if we only base our search on material goals or on absolute or absent opulence. No matter the immediate situation of the individual, there will always be a desire for something impossible, like the attempt to mix two worlds: the known and the unknown, the real and imaginary, and those worlds of gods and humans, lovers and concubines, husbands and cries, mists and gonads in vulvas.

... And when this is achieved, when each one searches and discovers why we exist, I will grab my boat and oars, and remembering all my lives condensed in one sole verse, I will penetrate the turbulent waters that angered the clouds and the evening winds, as an eternally black couple is sculpted into a rock that years ago possessed merry maidens who lived in cultural villages that disappeared, the dwellings of human heroes, today exalted.

And when I leave, you will remain, and in you, in some corner of your subconscious, the life I wanted and did not have will still be there: the life I desired and did not possess, the one I held and loathed, because it was not my life but the life of my parents and close neighbors, rivals and furtive lovers.

Baney (Bioko), 1991

Muffled Cries

It's those cries one drowns deep in one's throat when one ponders a curious event as immobile eyes or still figures appear. And this is what happens when we listen to history in verse narrated from archives of our idyllic Bubi community, life of yesterday and tomorrow, with moaning furtive beings as guests.

Reading the following verses, the listener will hear a distant reality, even though everything we find in them will remind us of familiar images. Like the exclamations upon having seen an old man or old woman naked, or the incontrollable cries of damsels and lovers as they hear the constant psalms emanating from the breath of composers of an erotic symphony. Old men, old women, the young and the adults, all live in moments of silence as they are obligated to muffle their cries in view of any situation no matter how harsh. This is the sense of "Muffled Cries."

Gritos plegados

Son esos gritos que uno ahoga en su garganta al contemplar un evento insólito cuando ante él desfilan ojos inmóviles o piezas inertes. Y eso es precisamente lo que sucede al escuchar en versos la historia que de nosotros nos cuentan los archiveros de nuestra comunidad idílica bubi, la vida de ayer y de mañana, teniendo en seres fugitivos y gimientes como huéspedes.

Al leer los versos que siguen, el oyente-lector encontrará una realidad lejana, aunque todo lo que en ellos perciba le remita a imágenes conocidas. Como las exclamaciones al ver a un anciano (o a una anciana) desnudo/a, o los gritos incontrolados de donceles y doncellas mientras escuchan salmos constantes que emanan del aliento de los autores de una sinfonía sexual. Ancianos o ancianas, jóvenes o adultos, todos ellos viven momentos de silencio en los que forzosamente han de plegar sus gritos ante cualquier situación, por muy dura que sea. Este es el sentido de los "Gritos plegados."

The Elder Böekka

They shall never again descend the mountains

Those noble men infused

In their irresistible fragrance.

And they shall set aside their fetid helmets,

Those who spilled the thick blood

Of the prey they once hunted.

They shall never again descend the mountains

Those haughty and possessed gentlemen

Whose message they brought to the Gods in the caves.

And the elder Baekkas will dance

As the damsels Baribèbi´ö sing

And men and women will dance

Without elixirs or adornments.

They shall no longer descend the mountains

Those noble warriors

Who lifted lances and battle axes,

And serpents and the meat of the conch.

And the weeds will grow in the cave

And the path will deceive,

And I shall sing hailing

The eternal departure of the Elder Böekka.

El anciano Böekka

No bajarán más de las montañas
Aquellos nobles imbuidos
En su irresistible fragancia.
Y dejarán sus hediondos cascos,
Aquellos que untaron con la sangre endrina
De las presas que una vez cazaron.
No bajarán más de las montañas
Aquellos altos y poseídos caballeros
Cuyo mensaje llevaron a los Dioses grutales.
Y bailarán los ancianos Baekka
Mientras cantan las doncellas Baribèbi´ö,
Y hombres y mujeres danzarán
Sin atavíos ni elixires.
No bajarán ya de las montañas
Aquellos nobles guerreros
Que subieron lanzas y hachas,
Y serpientes y carne desconchada.
Y crecerán las hierbas en la gruta
Y la senda mentirá,
Y cantaré anunciando
La eterna partida del anciano Böekka.

Servants Possessed

Flowering servants
Ancestral women possessed,
And figures encircled in the ground
With embraces and hanging bodies;
And the ancients possessed found repose
And the elder flowering women plowed the earth
In the boat of their massive buttocks,
And between chants and psalms,
Between surprise and astonishment
Their boat arrived at the pond,
And the elders possessed knelt down in front of them
As they danced the ballad of sex
And between cries and squeals
Men and women sang.
And you shall hear their song,
Not lustful,
Because this is how the dissolute damsels sang:
"è mmë ká tywikiriáé?
tywikíria a balë´é,
a batyapotyapo
i tyítya I óri"[1]
Flowering damsels and elder women possessed
In afternoons and mornings,
As men and gonads,
Reptiles and primates,
Gallants and ancients
Search anxiously,
For the boat of the women dancing ancestors.

---

1. Madame, what have we moved?
We have moved gonads,
Also phalluses,
The vulvas have matured.

Siervos poseídos

Siervas en flor

Ancestras poseídas,

Y figuras arqueadas en tierra

Con abrazos y cuerpos tendidos:

Y los ancianos poseídos hallaron cobijo

Y las ancestras en flor surcaron la tierra

En la barca de sus nalgas orondas,

Y entre cantos y salmos,

Entre asombros y sorpresas

Su barca arribó a la charca,

Y los ancianos poseídos se postraron ante ellas

Mientras danzaban la danza del sexo

Y entre gritos y gemidos

Hombres y mujeres cantaban.

Y oiréis su canto,

Mas no lujorioso,

Porque así cantaron las disolutas doncellas:

"è mmë ká tywikiriáé:

tywikíri a balë´é,

a batyapotyapo

i tyíria óri"[2]

Doncellas en flor y ancestras poseídas en tardes y alba,

Mientras hombres y gónadas,

Reptiles y társidos,

Donceles y ancianos buscan ansiosos,

La barca de las ancestras danzantes.

2. Señora, ¿qué hemos movido?
Hemos movido gónadas,
También falos,
Las vulvas maduraron.

Braided Life

Braided vines:

My wrists bleed

Because my ankles . . .

I neither stroll nor hurry.

Time and fire were witness

As the distilled aroma overtakes my garden,

And the glowing coals cry out in silence

Among the beings of the night muffling their sobs

As I open my eyes

And I see without looking

At my wrists bleeding

My fingers dance

My voice breaks:

I am no longer the warrior Böekka

Nor the old town crier

Nor the squirrel laying still in the vines.

I am no longer proud

Because I search for my center in the moist earth.

The beings of the night distract my gaze

As I dig and walk.

And my garden,

In the aroma and the smoke,

Engulfs hands and feet, and fingers, and fingers, and fingers.

Vida trenzada

Lianas trenzadas:
Y mis muñecas sangran
Porque mis tobillos . . .
Ni camino ni aprieto.
Tiempo y fuego fueron testigos
Mientras el aroma fermentado invade mi huerto,
Y los leños quemados gimen callados
En los seres de la noche que ocultan su llanto
Mientras abro mis ojos
Y veo sin mirar.
Mis muñecas sangran
Mis dedos danzan
Mi voz se quiebra:
Ya no soy el guerrero Böekka
Ni el anciano pregonero
Ni la ardilla quieta en las lianas.
Ya no estoy erguido
Porque busco mi estancia en la húmeda tierra.
Los seres de la noche distraen mi vista
Mientras cavo y camino
Y mi huerto,
Entre aromas y humos,
Acoge manos y pies, y dedos, y dedos, y dedos.

Ancestral Times

Where are those old times,
When the moon danced in the night
And your noble skin sang its song.

Where are the slow times,
When water possessed your noble body
And my fingers never strayed.

Where are the dreams' conclusions,
As voices narrated in the caves
The mysterious deeds of a mythical life gone by.

Where are the drowned voices,
As your sad eyes sang
The notes of a young gentleman.

Where is that life not lived,
When damsels and ancestors calmly awaited
Your arrival in the rocky paths.

Where is the waning night,
Where are the dreams' conclusions,
And where is that life not lived.

Tiempos de antaño

Dónde están los tiempos anclados,
Cuando la luna danzó en la noche
Y tu noble piel lució su canto.

Dónde están los tiempos pausados
Cuando el agua poseyó tu noble cuerpo
Y mis dedos jamás transitaron.

Dónde están los sueños conclusos,
Mientras las grutales voces narraban
Las misteriosas proezas de su ya mítica vida.

Dónde están las voces ahogadas,
Mientras tus ojos cantaban tristes
Los cantos del anciano doncel.

Dónde está la vida rehuida,
Cuando quietos en la gruta
Doncellas y ancestros aguardaban tu venida.

Dónde está la noche declinada,
Dónde están los sueños conclusos,
Y dónde está la vida rehuida.

The Last Lance

Today there is an offering from the cave-dwelling ancestors
As they sing disconsolate their destiny
In the sap and the vulva,
Among dances and rites:
Who shall bury the skillful warrior,
Who possesses the sad damsel
As furtive artists struggling in repose
Move and cry out?
Who buried the last lance?
And the ancestors narrate the bacchanal
The quiet life within you:
Broken braids in dances and cries
Eyes scrutinizing the missing night,
The buried Kyrie of the hoary ancestors,
Souls frantic within dancing bodies.
I shall dance in my frenzy the daring winds, and
I shall insert my fingers in pools of blood; and
The skin of your face shall be possessed
Even though the dawn dies for it; and
I shall adorn your body in the night as
I unleash the last battle,
Patiently waiting the Beauty of the Times.

La última lanza

Los ancestros grutales ofrendan hoy
Y cantan infaustos su destino
Entre savias y vulvas,
Entre danzas y ritos:
¿Quién entierra el hábil guerrero,
Quién posee a la triste doncella
Mientras transitan y calman
Divos furtivos en calma y lid?
¿Quién enterró ayer la última lanza?
Y los ancestros narran en bacanal
La callada vida que mora en ti?
Trenzas quebradas entre danzas y llantos
Ojos que escrutan la noche ausente,
Kirie enterrado de ancestros canos,
Almas que se agitan en cuerpos danzantes,
Bailaré afligido los osados aires, e
Inseriré mis dedos en charcas de sangre; y
La piel de tu rostro será poseída
Aunque por ello muera el alba; y
Ornaré tu cuerpo de la noche mientras
Libro en mí la última contienda,
Esperando quieto a la Bella de los Tiempos.

Afternoon Psalm

Let me stand as
I retrace my timeless steps;
Let my body rot
Standing in the earth,
And let my crown uncap the flow
That will fill my life of long ago,
As you lie in my bed
In desires and yearning,
In rejection and applause.
Let my tight shut eyes
Gaze without seeing;
Hidden in the ground that rises before them,
While the memory of one lone night of my restless past
Reappears in me.
Let me look feverishly for my body
Covered under the sheets
Of my long past refuge,
And today is my sacred tomb;
Let me quench my eternal thirst
With the sap I remove impatiently
From puddles and earth;
Let me strip skins
And sack villages in flight
And allow my staff to honor
Flowering damsels
Amidst the applause and the delirium
Amidst the longing and the tears,
Amidst desires and tenderness.

Let my soul wander

As my body breaks,

While they search for the narrator of my unsettled life,

The one with whom I shall tell the story

Of that damsel Bilaölé:

She of the boiling waters.

Let my tomb be my bed

And let my soul lie on top of me.

Let me search for the embrace

Among ancestors and sons,

Among damsels and tears,

In shadows and nights,

As I recall the slow dance

Of the damsel Bilaölé when,

Immersed in her sacred pulp,

I searched and I kept the secret of ancestors and earth.

El salmo del atardecer

Dejadme de pie mientras
Recorro sin tiempo mis caminos;
Dejad que mi cuerpo se pudra
De pie en la tierra,
Y que mi testa desprenda el efluvio
Que sahumará mi morada de antaño,
Mientras en mi lecho yaces
Entre anhelos y ansias,
Entre rechazos y aplausos.
Dejad que mis sellados ojos
Miren sin ver,
Ocultos por la tierra que ante ellos yergue,
Mientras en mí revive el recuerdo de sólo una noche
De mi agitada existencia.
Dejad que busque inquieto mi cuerpo
Cubierto ya bajo el lecho
De mi refugio de antaño,
Y que hoy es mi sacra tumba;
Dejad que sacie mi eterna sed
Con la savia que impaciente
Extraigo de pozas y tierra;
Dejad que huyendo desgarre pieles
Y destruya hogares
Y que mi cetro rinda honor
A doncellas en flor
Entre aplausos y delirios,
Entre ansias y lágrimas,
Entre deseos y ternura.

Dejad que mi alma vague
Mientras mi cuerpo se quiebra,
Mientras buscan al narrador de mi agitada vida,
Aquel con quien haré la historia
De aquella doncella Bilaölé:
La de las aguas hirvientes.
Dejad que mi tumba sea mi lecho
Y que sobre mí se pose mi alma;
Dejad que busque el abrazo
Entre ancestros y retoños,
Entre doncellas y lágrimas,
Entre sombras y noches,
Mientras recuerdo la danza callada
De la doncella Bilaölé, cuando
Agarrado a su sacra pulpa
Busqué y guardé el secreto de ancestros y tierra.

Before You

When my body lies still
And the fire of my hut lights the way,
When the remains of my body are only my body:
Stay.
Wait for my careful and furtive arrival
Without a thought for the times I intruded:
And contemplate the live shadow of the cold fire
As you take in my last breath.
And when all left of me is my body
Dwelling of beings and time
Stay.
I will see you because I'll be there,
Sitting or standing,
Stretched out or . . . ,
Because you will stay.

Antes que tú

Cuando mi cuerpo yazga inerte
Y el fuego de mi choza te alumbre,
Cuando de mi cuerpo no quede más que cuerpo:
Quédate.
Aguarda mi cauta y furtiva venida
Sin mirar cuántas veces invadí tu morada:
Y contempla la sombra viva del fuego frío
Mientras acoges mi último suspiro.
Y cuando de mí no quede más que cuerpo
Morada de seres y tiempo
Quédate.
Y yo te veré porque allí seguiré,
Sentado o de pie,
Tendido o . . . :
Porque tú te habrás quedado.

Ö ma löe (The Goodbye)

And the young men shall carry him dressed in decorum
Coming and going in cries and blows;
And the damsels shall see him
The hoary warrior they once knew.
Who tells of his glories,
Who talks to him of now,
Who searches for him when
In forests and seas
He consumes meat of the conch?

And the gentleman shall carry his jolting body,
And the warriors shall protect it,
And the earth shall possess him;
And from there the seed shall sprout
Giving life to his offspring.
"Take me away now," the gentleman warrior shall cry.
"Take me now as I move silent,
As damsels and little ones sing of me;
Take me to those whom I carried yesterday
And tell them that I shall go
When I see without eyes,
When I speak to you voiceless,
When I live something not-life,
When stretched out and still
Moving in front of me
Appear my lovers and victims."

Ö ma löe (El Adios)

Y los donceles le portarán ataviado
Yendo y viniendo entre gritos y golpes:
Y las doncellas verán entre canas
Al viejo guerrero que una vez conocieron.
¿Quién narra sus glorias,
Quién le habla de hogaño,
Quién le busca cuando entre bosques y mares
Consume carne desconchada?

Y los donceles le portarán atajado,
Y los guerreros guardarán su cuerpo
Y la tierra le poseerá;
Y de ella brotará la semilla que dará aliento a su retoño.
"Llevadme corriendo," dirá el guerrero doncel,
"Llevadme mientras transito callado,
Mientras por mí cantan doncellas y retoños;
Llevadme entre aquellos que ayer llevé
Y decidles que yo iré
Cuando vea sin ojos,
Cuando os hable sin voz,
Cuando viva sin ser la vida,
Cuando tendido y quieto
Transiten ante mí
Aquellos de quienes amante y verdugo fui."

Misty Waters

And I will sing her life in the night

As long as the crickets,

Hidden in flames, cease to sing.

And I will expose the life of the circumcised gentlemen

Who bravely wander searching,

As the Gods and ancestors dance.

And I will tell of the steps they took in lagoons

As I contemplate their eternal face,

When she-wolves and squirrels

Embrace the shadow of the night.

And I will watch over their steps

As her song fades in the rocks

Those whom she watched in my absence;

And she will walk among still giants

Or in misty waters,

When the crickets announce

The water of the silent rocks.

And she will be the wilted flower

That bloomed yesterday in the sacred cave,

Where Gods and Ancestors embraced the night.

Aguas en bruma

Y cantaré su vida en la noche
Mientras callan los lapados grillos
Que las llamas ocultan.
Y revelaré la vida que buscan osados
Los circuncisos donceles que vagan,
Mientras danzan dioses y ancestros.
Y contaré sus huellas en charcas
Mientras contemple su eterna faz,
Cuando lobas y ardillas
Abrazan la sombra de la noche.
Y guardaré sus pasos
Mientras fallece su canto en las rocas
Aquellas que ayer miró en mi ausencia;
Y caminará entre gigantes quietos
O entre aguas en bruma,
Cuando los grillos anuncien
El agua de las rocas que callan.
Y ella será la flor marchita
Que ayer brotó en la sagrada cueva,
Donde Dioses y Ancestros abrazaron la noche.

The Ancestral Dance

Dancing

With your body

The ancestral dance;

And your mouth will set

The beat with the claps

Of gentlemen and damsels,

Or old keepers of the hidden secret.

And with your song I will discover

Deeds of times gone by,

When death was nothing

But a restful break

That will return to its fleeting journey,

Or when God and I taste you,

And you arch your figure

When I possess you,

And mud and dust shine your skin;

And you will speak as they spoke long ago

In caves and sacred dwellings;

And you will tell what memory has buried

For I shall be your song and your body,

Your eyes and your steps,

Your memory and your life.

I shall be the time encased in you,

While you dance without restraint

The old dance of Gods and ancestors.

El baile ancestral

Y con tu cuerpo bailaré

La danza ancestral;

Y tu boca moldeará

El ritmo que aplauden

Jóvenes donceles y doncellas,

O viejos poseedores del secreto oculto.

Y con tu canto descubriré

Hechos acaecidos en el tiempo,

Cuando la muerte era sin más

El reposo temporal de aquellos que

Debería volver de su fugaz periplo,

O cuando Dios y yo te catamos.

Y arquearás tu figura

Cuando yo te posea,

Y barro y polvo lucirán tu piel;

Y hablarás como lo hicieron antaño

En grutas y sagradas chozas;

Y contarás lo que las memorias entierran

Porque yo seré tu canto y tu cuerpo,

Tus ojos y tus pasos,

Tu memoria y tu vida.

Seré el tiempo en ti poseído,

Mientras danzas sin pudor

La lejana danza de Dioses y ancestros.

The Last Damsel

And as I confuse my gaze in your eyes
Beings appear before me
Whose psalms long ago
Told of the bitter existence
Of that last virginal damsel
Whose flower no one saw or possessed.
And I will share my lustful dwelling
With those who, like me,
Live immersed in the dark abysm
Of the life they silently carve.
With my gaze in your eyes
I observe in fog and tears,
The dark image born
Of the possessed gentleman's psalm
Announcing his interrupted stay.
I contemplated the last damsel
Dawning her ornate robes,
Whose life and glory were sung:
Bones and bracelets adorn her legs,
Bones and shells her arms,
Skins and lotions embellish her thighs
When the fog nourishes the water
Running through the hills and crevices.
The haughty damsels will descend at dusk
And they will hear the waters filling
Their sacred mortal lagoons;
And by sunset they will rise,
Dampened by ancestors

And before me they will pass

And I will contemplate the last damsel

Possessed by mist and waters,

And in her womb she will keep

The song and the tears

Recalling the ancestors, damsels of the past.

And in the fire and mist

In bones and conches

Or in hills and lagoons

Sad and silent I will sing

As she did,

The ballad of the last damsel:

"tyuè tö la bòlá bí tyë

i tyë tá aná tywë bëtéò´e,

tyuè tö la bòlá bí tyë

i tyë tá aná tywë bëlla."[3]

---

3. We are children of the world
The world knows not that we are roosters
We are children of the world
The world knows not that we sing.

La última doncella

Y mientras confundo mi mirada en tus ojos
Ante mí yerguen seres
Que antaño narraron en salmos
La amarga existencia
De aquella última y virginal doncella
Cuya flor nadie vio ni poseyó.
Y compartiré mi lujuriosa morada
Con aquellos que, como yo,
Viven inmersos en el oscuro abismo
De la vida que esculpen callados.
Con mi mirada en tus ojos
Observo, entre niebla y lágrimas,
La oscura imagen nacida
Del salmo del doncel poseído
Que anuncia su ya quebrada estancia.
Contemplé a la última doncella
Ataviada y ornada,
Cuya vida y gloria cantaron las romanzas:
Tabas y anillos adornan sus piernas,
Tabas y conchas decoran sus brazos,
Pieles y ungüentos florean en sus caderas
Cuando la niebla fecunda las aguas
Que recorren montes y brechas.
Al alba bajarán las doncellas infantas
Y escucharan las aguas que mañana llenarán
Sus sagradas y mortales pozas;
Y por el ocaso subirán,
Y serán rociadas por ancestros

Y ante mí pasarán.

Y contemplaré a la última doncella

Que brumas y agua poseyeron,

Y guardará en sus entrañas

El canto y las lágrimas que recordarán

Las ancestras ayer doncellas.

Y entre fuego y bruma,

Entre tabas y conchas

O entre montes y pozas

Cantaré triste y callado

La romanza que cantó la última doncella:

"tyuè tö la bòlá bí tyë

I tyë tá aná tywë bëtéò ´e,

Tyuè tö la bòlá bí tyë

I tyë tá aná tywë bëlla."[4]

---

[4]. Nosotros somos hijos del mundo
El mundo ignora que somos gallos
Nosotros somos hijos del mundo
El mundo ignora que cantamos.

The Boatman's Song

è maálé!
è maálé!
è maálé!

Sang the boatman
As your boat faded away
Furrowing the misty sea,
As his voice softened in the fog
And rain drowned his skin:

è maálé!
è maálé!
è maálé!

And the God Riobáttá roared
In the frosty mist
Of the oarsmen guiding the distant gentleman
As in the old times,
Who pursues my woman,
Who calls at my dwelling
Who approaches me?
And as your voice loved the thunder
The furtive mist possessed you,
And I furrowed the seas
In search of the damsel
Once possessed
By the misty waters:

è maálé!
è maálé!
è maálé! . . .

El canto del barquero

è maálé!
è maálé!
è maálé!

Y así gritaba el barquero
Mientras tu barca se alejaba
Surcando la mar en bruma,
Mientras su voz se perdía en la niebla
Y la lluvia ahogaba su piel:

è maálé!
è maálé!
è maálé!

Y el Dios Riobáttá rugió
Entre la gélida bruma
Que antaño rasgaron
Los barqueros guías del doncel lejano:
¿Quién acosa a mi zagala,
Quién llama a mi morada,
Quién posa a mi vera?
Y mientras tu voz amaba el trueno
La bruma te poseía furtiva,
Y yo surcaba las mares
En busca de la doncella
Que las aguas en bruma
Una vez poseyeron:

è maálé!
è maálé!
è maálé! . . .

The Beauty of All Time

Tèète, Tèète
Sibébá, Sibébá,
Sibulabötyö,
Tö la utyë Rèrè
Tö té wèlla.[5]

As I stroll and sing
I break the lances of life and death,
When night becomes eternal
And hidden in the daylight
Is the Damsel who crossed the threshold of time.
I go in search, I say,
Of the Beauty of All Time.
You can find her standing on a rock, they say,
As the damsels dance, still,
In the lagoon,
And their moist bodies shine
In the salt and the water
And the bile of their tears and elixir;
You will find her anointed with the sacred substance
They say, of Goddesses and Damsels and Ancestors.
I search for the Beauty of All Time,
She whom no one found
The Beauty of yonder,
Where no one goes
And no one searches,
Where dwells the Beauty of All Time.

---

5. Tééte, Tééte
Little hunter, little hunter
People's protector
We are searching Rèrè
We have not seen her.

La Bella de los Tiempos

Tèète, Tèète
Sibébá, Sibébá,
Sibulabötyö,
Tö la utyë Rèrè
Tö té wèlla.⁶

Camino y canto mientras
Quiebro las lanzas de la vida y la muerte,
Cuando la noche se vuelve eterna
Y el día oculta entre su luz
A la Doncella que cruzó el umbral de los tiempos.
Voy en busca, digo,
De la Bella de los Tiempos.
La hallarás posada en la roca, dicen,
Mientras las doncellas danzan, quietas,
En la poza
Y sus húmedos cuerpos brillan
Entre la sal del agua
Y la hiel de sus lágrimas y elixir;
La hallarás untada con la sagrada sustancia
Dicen, de Diosas y Doncellas y Ancestros.
Voy en busca de la Bella de los Tiempos,
Aquella a la que nadie halló jamás
Aquella Bella de allí,
Donde nadie va
Y donde nadie busca,
Donde mora la Bella de los Tiempos.

---

6. Tèète, Tèète
Pequeño cazador, pequeño cazador
Protector del pueblo
Buscamos a Rèrè
No la hemos visto.

Image and Blood

Uncertain images,
Cries and moans heralding
Fire and tears,
Cries in mortal embraces
Of dark bodies in the black night;
Images that today recall
The loathed life
Of a tomorrow that will not come.

Night weeps and sings
And cries,
And your fire burns me,
Because this is why you were created,
To reveal the Gods' and Ancestors' prophecy:
"And she shall burn and embrace
The man who explores her,
And we shall follow
In the caves and the lagoons
In dances and songs
Sealing with embers the burnt bodies."
Sad images
Of grey fire and clear flesh:
I will tint my blunt teeth
And smear my dark teeth
With your dark blood,
While you, crying and dancing,
Burn my dark skin,
With your clear body ...

Imagen y sangre

Imágenes inciertas,
Gemidos y gritos que anuncian
Fuego y lágrimas,
Llantos entre mortales abrazos
De cuerpos oscuros en la negra noche;
Imágenes que hoy recuerdan
La odiada vida
Que mañana no será.

La noche canta entre llantos
Y gritos
Y tu fuego me abrasa,
Porque así te hicieron
Para que se cumpla el oráculo de Dioses y Ancestros;
"Y abrasará entre abrazos
Al hombre que la explore,
Y surgiremos de grutas y pozas
Entre danzas y cantos
Sellando con ascuas los abrasados cuerpos."
Tristes imágenes
De fuego gris en carne clara:
Teñiré mis desafilados dientes
Con tu sangre muerta,
Y con ella regaré mi oscura faz
Mientras, entre llantos y danzas,
Abrasas mi oscura piel
Con tu cuerpo claro . . .

Pool of Tears

I need to ask you forgiveness
But I don't know who you are or why.
I need to kneel down before you
Because without my intention
I shadowed your progress.
I need to pause and look at you
And see, silent before you,
The time I was
Or, as they say, the one I will be,
Perhaps then I shall shed that tear
That will give you strength to deliver me
Pray for pain
Pray for passion
That blow I'm waiting for
As I kneel before you.
I need to gather myself, as I narrate
The deeds that yesterday made you believe
But today, with a tardy glance,
You lift and cover my earthy body.
I need to ask forgiveness
And kneel down before you
With my afflicted mind,
Because I was what some did
And what others said.
Now in serenity I contemplate
The damsels you watch over,
And I tell my life in pools
While at the end of the day
You await my arrival.

Charca lacrimal

Necesito pedirte perdón
Pero no sé quién eres ni por qué.
Necesito postrarme ante ti
Porque sin desearlo
Fui la sombra que eclipsó tu marcha.
Necesito mirarte quieto
Y ver callado en ti el tiempo que fui
O tal como dicen, aquel que seré,
Tal vez así derrame esa lágrima
Que te dará fuerza para asestarme
Ora por dolor
Ora por pasión
El golpe que aguardo
Ante ti postrado.
Necesito fundirme, mientras narro
Los hechos que ayer te hicieron creer
Pero que hoy,
Con mirada tardía,
Recoges y cubres mi terroso cuerpo.
Necesito pedirte perdón
Y postrarme ante ti
Con mi mente alterada,
Porque fui lo que unos hicieron
Y lo que otros dijeron.
Ahora contemplo quieto
A doncellas por ti veladas,
Y narro mi vida en charcas
Mientras en tarde y alba
Aguardas quieta mi llegada.

The Goddess Löbëla

Löbëla is Wewèöpö, Wésëpa, Úri; she is the love goddess mother. She is our mother goddess, but she is also the man god who irreverently scratches like a young gentleman in a hurry. Löbëla is the ancient husband trickster who discovered the brides-to-be in the red waters of the lagoon; Löbëla is the old woman who never stepped on the ground, the guide of women young and old, the queen of the god Wedye. In turn she is the lover of who-knows-what furtive god who appears out of the shadows of the dwelling of Sítòböro. But . . . who is Löbëla?

La ondina Löbëla

Löbëla es Wewèöpó, es Wésëpa, es Úri; es la diosa amante y madre. También es nuestra diosa madre, y a su vez el dios hombre que posee y desgarra impío cual joven doncel apresurado. Es el marido y anciano trepador que descubrió a las doncellas casaderas poseídas en la poza de las teñidas aguas rojas; es la anciana cuyos pies nunca pisaron el suelo, la guía de mujeres y zagalas, la reina del dios Wedye. Es a su vez amante de no sé qué furtivo dios llegado de las tinieblas donde mora Sítòböro. Pero . . . ¿quién es Löbëla?

Dust and Moon

Dust:

Between sweat and flow

On the rise, implacable

From kicks and mud and earth,

Legs and earth fornicating

In screams

Under the mortal rays of the watching Sun.

Suffering I pour sobs

In the hollow sun baked rock

That always waited for the vile moment,

As you contemplate deliriously

My spent existence . . .

Years gone by, the crickets sang

Today,

In bitter passion

They weep

The ones who yesterday screamed

Beneath the bundle of the drowned moon . . .

Red and moon

And legs and earth:

The crickets sing when you silence

What your body tells:

And it says it emerged from dust

And blows

Polvo y luna

Polvo:
Entre sudores y efluvios
Asciende implacable
Desde los golpes de piernas y barro y tierra,
Piernas y tierra fornican
Entre gritos
Bajo los mortales rayos del Sol testigo.
Vierto mis agónicos llantos
En la candente y hueca roca
Que siempre aguardó el vil momento,
Mientras deliras y contemplas
Mi carcomida existencia...
Antaño cantaron los grillos
Hoy,
Entre amargas pasiones
Lloran los grillos
Que ayer gritaron
Bajo el haz que fue de la luna ahogada...
Rojo y luna
Y piernas y tierra:
Los grillos cantan cuando callas
Lo que tu cuerpo canta,
Y cuenta que surgió entre polvos
Y golpes

The Versed Path

I went walking dragged

Into fire and ponds

Pouring my grain in baked mud

And that's as it was.

I walked surrounded by fog and tears,

By ponds and ashes,

And I spoke because I wished to tell stories,

I tell stories because I want to be silent:

"And he walked aimlessly years ago

Broken, no direction

And he walked without feet prostrate in the mud

In fire and ponds

Searching along the way

For what he found yesterday."

I walk uncertain

Among blows and cries

Because my Goddess remained behind.

El camino en verso

Y caminé arrastrado

Entre fuego y charcas

Posando mi grano en barro ya cocido:

Y así fue.

Y caminé envuelto entre niebla y llantos,

Entre charcas y cenizas,

Y hablé porque quise contar,

Cuento porque quiero callar:

"Y caminó errante antaño

Desviado y quebrado,

Y caminó sin pies posado en el lodo

Entre fuego y charcas

Buscando lo que ayer halló en el camino."

Yo camino incierto

Entre golpes y llantos

Porque mi Diosa se quedó atrás.

Song

I sing destiny risen
In altering hills
Someone formed years ago;
I wish to imbibe my broken life
And return inside the humid earth
Which gave birth to that dark seed.

I want the flower that resists
The drops of hard rain imprisoning
The crude and fearless villagers;
My body no longer gives in
Now that within me
Hangs the weight of altering hills.
Where is life,
And for whom,
As the Goddess Löbëla
Goes back to her eternal departure?
For whom to live
When the hills open up,
When rocks break,
When the lagoon is no longer wet?
I sing destiny risen
In altering hills
And I sing loud the name of Löbëla
As your image overtakes my mind.

El canto

Canto el sino crecido
Entre montes cambiantes
Que alguien asió desde hace tiempo;
Deseo ingerir mi quebrada existencia
Y volver a la húmeda tierra
Que fecundó aquella semilla oscura.

Anhelo la flor que resiste
Los golpes de las lluvias que recluyen
A los desabridos e impávidos aldeanos;
Mi cuerpo ya no transige
Desde que llevo en mí
El peso de montes cambiantes.
¿Dónde está la vida,
Y para quién se vive,
Mientras la Diosa Löbëla
Recula en su perpetua partida?
Para quién se vive
Cuando los montes se agrietan,
Cuando la húmeda charca calla?
Cuando las rocas se quiebran,
Canto el sino crecido
Entre montes cambiantes
Y grito con mi canto el nombre de Löbëla
Mientras tu imagen se funde en mi mente.

Wésëpa!

Wésëpa!
The Town will cry out your name
As you carry within you
The seed of God father and consort;
Damsels shall sing your name
As deep within you lies
The son who shall clasp lances and torches:
Wésëpa!

Your name shall ring out
In shadows and depths,
In seas and hills;
As man,
Your God
Will witness the decline of man
Yesterday aided by the beings of the earth;
Your God will cry out your name
And will watch over the live ones walking
As we remember the icons of our existence,
And I will receive the aid of guttural forces
When the cobra rises up before me
His gaze nailed in my pupil
While vapors rise from my head
The boa's crown lies restlessly
Jealously hiding her body.
And clasping my staff
I shall reign for decades
And then,

The cobra's gaze shall dim,
The boa's crown shall fall
And flutes and horns shall sound
From the river Eökö's plaza,
And the wild damsels Baribèbi´ö
Shall take hold of staffs, lances and axes
Buried by Baekka elders.
Thunder and cries will sound,
Songs and sobs
And fire and blood shall cover men and earth
And the young shall emerge
And we shall adore Gods and Ancestors,
And we shall walk tall
Undaunted,
That is how we shall live.

Wésëpa!

Wésëpa!
El Pueblo gritará tu nombre
Mientras lleves en ti
La semilla del Dios padre y consorte;
Las doncellas cantarán tu nombre
Mientras tus entrañas guarden
Al hijo que asirá lanchas y antorchas:
Wésëpa!

Será tu nombre el que se escuche
En tinieblas y abismos,
En mares y montes;
Será tu Dios quien
Como hombre,
Contemple el declive del hombre
Ayer asistido por seres de la tierra;
Tu Dios gritará tu nombre
Y velará por los vivos caminantes
Mientras recordemos nuestra mítica existencia.
Y seré asistido por las fuerzas grutales
Cuando la cobra se irga ante mí
Con la mirada clavada en mi pupila
Mientras sobre mi cabeza humeante
Reposará la testa de la boa insumisa
Que celosa oculta su cuerpo.
Y con mi cetro empuñado
Reinaré doce lustros
Y entonces,

La mirada de la cobra se apagará,
La testa de la boca caerá
Y sonarán pitos y flautas
Desde la plaza del río Eökö,
Y las indomables doncellas Baribèbi´ö
Empuñarán los cetros, las lanzas y las hachas
Que ayer enterraron los ancianos Baekka.
Sonarán truenos y gritos,
Cantos y llantos
Y fuego y sangre cubrirán hombres y tierra
Y brotarán nuevos retoños
Y adoraremos Dioses y Ancestros,
Y caminaremos erguidos
Impávidos,
Porque viviremos así.

Hollows and Hills

I seek the smooth white elixir
That flows from warm pools
Between skin and blood;
I seek the established life of
My haughty Ancestors decorated
With the unsettled blood the Gods did not drink;
I search the eternal pleasure well kept
In the deep trenches and hills
Between hatchet blows and mortal reptiles;
I ingest mixed blood in the night
As a thirsty God
Because I do not want and I possess
Because I do not search and I find:
Trenches and pools
And tombs of reptiles and Ancestors
Who drank until drunk that smooth white elixir
Of life and death,
Of hills and palms,
Of hatchets and conches,
Of heads and tails
From up, from down.
I seek because I possess
And I possess because I want,
And I want because I do not find
Always trapped in deep and dark caverns,
Because there I was engendered
And there I found the life I quickly consume,
And there they will keep my remains
When I search and do not find,
When I want and do not possess,
When I cease to absorb at night

Hoyos y montes

Busco el blanco y suave elixir
Que germina de la cálida y encharcada poza
Entre piel y sangre;
Busco la vida que ayer sembraron
Mis pedantes Ancestros decorados
Con la descompuesta sangre que no bebieron los Dioses;
Busco el eterno gozo que guardan, celosas,
Las profundas zanjas de golpes
Entre montes de hachas y mortales reptiles;
Ingiero sangre confusa en la noche
Cuan sediento Dios
Porque no quiero y poseo,
Porque no busco y hallo:
Zanjas y charcas
Y tumba de reptiles y Ancestros
Que bebieron en exceso el blanco y suave elixir
De vida y muerte,
De montes y palmas,
De hachas y conchas,
De testas y colas
Desde arriba, desde abajo.
Busco porque poseo
Y poseo porque quiero,
Y quiero porque no hallo
Siempre atrapado en la caverna oscura y honda,
Porque en ella fui engendrado
Y en ella hallé la vida que presto consumo,
Y en ella guardarán mis restos
Cuando busque y no halle,
Cuando desee y no posea,
Cuando cese de absorber de noche

Versed Secrets

I live in pleasure and lust, as
Phallic tongues
Penetrate that mysterious, and
Dark deep hole where, today
Infants' hearts beat.
I ponder and keep watch in trickling cracks,
I remember that years ago I found and consumed
Boldly,
Like a running beast,
Hungry and thirsty.
I prepare my well-worn climbing rings,
I anoint my hills and polluted rivers;
I trace the path on which tomorrow
We will fuse hearts and tongues
All stretched and shaken,
Hidden in rivers and hills.
I tell of what I always was:
An intruder lascivious with glances and verses,
Nectar hidden in laughter and tears,
Like a young wife overtaken
By a still unrepentant husband,
Perverse and virile.
I hide still in the mist and cracks
Nourishment of damsels and ancestors
Oracle of the great and the small,
Serpent of lagoons and forests,
Dwelling of those who do not rest
And the dream of those who dream eternally.

Secretos versados

Entre placeres y lujuria vivo, mientras
Lenguas fálicas
Calan en ese misterioso y, también
Oscuro y abismal hoyo donde, hoy
Laten corazones infantes.
Pienso y aguardo entre brechas goteantes,
Recuerdo que antaño hallé y consumí
Osado,
Cuan fiera en vela,
Sediento y hambriento.
Templo mis aros ya marchitos,
Incienso mis montes y ríos hediondos;
Trazo la senda por la que mañana
Uniremos lenguas y corazones
Todos desencajados y estirados,
Ocultos entre ríos y montes.
Cuento lo que siempre fui:
Intruso y perverso con miradas y versos,
Néctar oculto entre risas y llantos,
Cuan joven esposa violada por su todavía
Osado esposo, perverso y varonil.
Aguardo quieto entre brumas y grutas
Cuan pitanza de doncellas y ancestros,
Oráculo de grandes y chicos,
Serpiente de pozas y bosques,
Morada de aquellos que no descansan
Y sueño de aquellos que sueñan eternamente.

Löbëla

Löbëla

Goddess emerging from dark clay

Diligently self-sculpted

Shaping her sacred

And still tender body.

Löbëla,

Nymph of regal gait

And breasts warm yesterday

With fingers and tongues and teeth.

Löbëla,

Goddess sculpting desired limbs

Passing through a short path

Between tongues and lips;

Legs running through trails

That yesterday traversed the Gods and Nobel Baekkas

Searching for flowering damsels

In long breasts and rolling braids

That I, a petty god of flesh and pleasure,

Hid in the lagoon of the young Wewèöpö.

Löbëla,

Goddess who carves and sings

Goddess of slow steps

Goddess of scrawny limbs,

Löbëla,

She of long sacred breasts,

Young Goddess of spongy lips,

Those visible and invisible,

Lips desired when hidden,

The Mother-Goddess Löbëla sculpts
As she narrates her destiny:
"You shall walk and you shall find your name
But you shall return."
And the Goddess Löbëla emerged from the clay
To grow and become desired
By those living and the ancestors,
By Gods and humans,
By men and by the young
In legends and stories:
Löbëla!

Löbëla

Löbëla
Diosa que brota de la oscura arcilla
Por ella misma esculpida con esmero
Dando forma a su sacro santo
Y todavía tierno cuerpo.
Löbëla,
Diosa de andares ondinos
Y pechos ayer templados
Con dedos y lenguas y dientes
Löbëla,
Diosa que esculpe las añoradas piernas
Con las que recorre el corto camino
Entre lenguas y labios;
Piernas que recorren aquellos caminos
Que antaño pisaron los Dioses y Nobles Baekka
En busca de las jóvenes en flor
De pechos largos y trenzas revueltas
Que yo,
Nimio dios de carne y placer,
Oculté en la poza de la doncella Wewèöpö.
Löbëla,
Diosa que esculpe y canta
Diosa de andares pausados
Diosa de piernas "yantadas."
Löbëla,
La de los pechos largos y sacros,
Joven Diosa de labios en pulpa,
Los visibles y los invisibles,

Labios que ocultos son codiciados.
La Madre-Diosa Löbëla esculpe
Mientras narra su propio destino:
"Caminarás y encontrarás tu nombre
Pero volverás."
Y la Diosa Löbëla brotó de la arcilla
Para crecer y ser codiciada
Por vivos y ancestros,
Por Dioses y humanos,
Por hombres y púberes
Entre leyenda y cuentos:
¡Löbëla!

The Ballad of Löbëla

Tears drop from an afflicted god
And fall in a dark cavern
Where they ferment to impregnate
The moist earth of sun and fire.
And from tears and earth rises
The walking goddess whom no one names,
Her feet hidden by rings of mist
That soften her quiet steps.
Oh, walking goddess of cavernous earth,
Oh, Goddess of earthly trails
You who soothed the afflicted god
And converted his tears to mystery and earth!
Who could have conceived your arrival,
Who could have molded your sacred body
But the guttural gods who loved you
When you emerged from your sacred womb?
And they tell.
They tell of the walking goddess who was the old climber
Who discovered the young damsels of the God Ebi´ö,
That it was also the walking goddess,
The one called Wewèöpö,
The beauty of the hills and mountains.
They say the old climber called the walking goddess
Löbëla, whose tired feet in the misty rings
Never stepped on the earth.
And they tell of the walking goddess Wewèöpö
Sung of herself when she climbed her sacred palm tree,
While below she danced in red waters.

And the walking goddess was called Löbëla,
And Wewèöpö,
And Úri,
And Kölekkò.
And the walking goddess bloodied her palm tree
And the walking goddess dyed her waters red
And she was possessed by the old climber
To end the chaos of Mööga
I tell it as long as someone listens,
I tell the mysterious life of Löbëla and Wewèöpö.
The life of Úri and Kölekkò;
I tell the life of Sóbòole and Möhókó
And I tell the story of what no one could bury
Because I tell and sing the Ballad of Löbëla.

La balada de Löbëla

Las lágrimas de un afligido dios se esparcen

Y caen en una oscura caverna

Donde se fermentan para fecundar

La acuosa tierra de soles y fuegos.

Y entre lágrimas y tierra surge

La caminante diosa que nadie nombra,

Diosa caminante de pies en bruma

Envueltos en ocultos rodetes

Que amortiguan sus callados pasos.

¡Oh caminante diosa de cavernal tierra,

Oh diosa de humanos andares

Que calmaste al afligido dios

Y convertiste sus lágrimas en misterio y tierra!

¿Quién contempló tu llegada,

Quién moldeó tu sacro cuerpo

Sino grutales dioses que te amaron

Cuando saliste de tus sacras entrañas?

Y cuentan.

Cuentan que la diosa caminante fue el anciano trepador

Que descubrió a las jóvenes del Dios Ebi´ö

Y que fue también la diosa caminante

La doncella que todos llamaron Wewèöpö,

Bella de colinas y montes.

Cuentan que el anciano trepador llamó a Löbëla

A la diosa caminante cuyos pies sobre rodetes,

Jamás posaron en tierra.

Y cuentan que la caminante diosa Wewèöpö

Se cantó cuando trepaba su sacra palmera,

Mientras abajo danzaba en las aguas rojas.

Y la caminante diosa se llamó Löbëla,

Y también se llamó Wewèöpö

Y Úri,

Y Kölekkò.

Y la caminante Diosa sangró su palmera

Y la caminante diosa tiñó de rojo sus aguas

Y fue poseída por el anciano trepador

Para parar el caos de Mööga

Yo cuento mientras alguien escuche,

Cuento la misteriosa vida de Löbëla y Wewèöpö,

La vida de Úri y Kölekkò;

Cuento la vida de Sóbòole y Möhókó

Y narro lo que nadie logró enterrar

Porque cuento y canto la Balada de Löbëla.

Löbëla and Úri

E wá Löbëla, e wá Löbëlö
E wá Löbëla, e wá Löbëlö
Ëtyuppo tyi nóö ′ia
E bëebba e yööbö
Ö bötúkku e orí i tyé la baölë
Mwè e bara Úri
A bara Löbëla[7]

And the Master of Times arrived
One time Master and Lord
Of lands and seas:
And he possessed Úri
And he possessed Löbëla;
Úri was queen and mother
Löbëla goddess and lover.
Löbëla wandered aimlessly
When the Master of Times
Returned to his lands and seas.
Whom does Löbëla search,
Whom does Úri contemplate?
And the Master of Times arrived
Once Lord and Master
Of lands and seas;
And he thrust his force in the entrials of Úri

7. Löbëla, Löbëla
Löbëla, Löbëla,
The storm does not allow me to hear
The master of lands and people,
Married Úri
He married Löbëla.

And he searched for Löbëla in depths and darkness:
And she said:
"Do not look for me, do not possess me,
I was possessed in your absence."
And Löbëla was repudiated and loved
Ever wandering.
And now she walks barefoot
In sobs and mist
In search of the grotto where
Gods and mortals meet,
The living and the wandering,
The dead and the believing,
Pagans and mothers.
The Master of Times possessed Úri,
The Master of Times repudiated Löbëla.
Löbëla shouted and searched,
The Master of Times possessed Úri,
The Master of Times loved Löbëla.

Löbëla y Úri

E wá Löbëla, e wá Löbëlö

E wá Löbëla, e wá Löbëlö

Ëtyuppo tyi nóö ´ia

E bëebba e yööbö

Ö bötúkku e orí i tyé la baölë

Mwè e bara Úri

A bara Löbëla[8]

Y llegó el Señor de los tiempos

Una vez señor y Dueño

De tierras y mares:

Y poseyó a Úri

Y poseyó a Löbëla;

Úri fue reina y madre

Löbëla fue diosa y amante.

Löbëla caminó errante

Cuando el Señor de los Tiempos

Regresó a sus tierras y mares.

¿A quién busca Löbëla,

A quién contempla Úri?

Y llegó el Señor de los Tiempos

Una vez Señor y Dueño

De tierras y mares;

8. Löbëla, Löbëla,
Löbëla, Löbëla
El chaparrón me impide escuchar
Las olas son muy fuertes
El señor de tierras y personas
Se casó con Úri
Esposó a Löbëla.

Y posó su fuerza en el seno de Úri

Y buscó a Löbëla en abismos y tinieblas:

"No me busques ni me poseas," dijo Löbëla,

"En tu ausencia fui poseída."

Y Löbëla fue repudiada y amada

Siempre errante.

Y ahora camina descalza

Entre llantos y niebla

En busca de la gruta donde se juntan y acuden

Dioses mortales,

Vivos y errantes,

Difuntos y creyentes,

Paganos y madres.

El Señor de los Tiempos poseyó a Úri,

El Señor de los Tiempos repudió a Löbëla.

Löbëla llamó y buscó,

El Señor de los Tiempos poseyó a Úri,

El Señor de los Tiempos amó a Löbëla.

Hidden Heat

Who burns me,
And who consumes all of me
When floating through my head
Lingers the sculpted round flesh
Of the Goddess whom I once adored?
Who consumes me,
Who burns me bodily
While the memory of what I once was
Travels through my destiny?
Who discovers my dwelling
In fortune and glory,
In remembrances and flesh,
In tears and carnal desires?
Who burns and consumes me,
Laments and sheds tears,
Observes and pleads,
Licks and repudiates
Throws stones and tears,
Covers and exposes?
Who cries out my name,
Who oppresses my soul
In shouts and tears?
Who possesses and drags me?
And who burns me?

La oculta candencia

¿Quién me abrasa,
Y quién me consume en cuerpo
Cuando por mi mente transita
El arqueado cuerpo esculpido
De la diosa que antaño adoré?
¿Quién me consume,
Quién me abrasa en cuerpo
Mientras en mi sino transita
El recuerdo que fue?
¿Quién descubre mi morada
Entre dichas y glorias,
Entre recuerdos en carne,
Entre lujurias y llantos?
¿Quién me abrasa y consume,
Lamenta y llora,
Observa y ruega
Lame y repudia,
Lapida y desgarra,
Arropa y expone?
¿Quién grita mi nombre,
Quién oprime mi alma
Entre gritos y llantos?
¿Quién me posee y arrastra?
¿Y quién me abrasa?

Cries and Laughter

My eyes seek
What your body delivers,
When in steps and blows
The dance of skeletal ancestors
Comes alive in you.
I look and listen
What your body sings
When in cries and laughter
You tell the legend in you
I sang yesterday.
I touch and observe
What no one sees now in you,
Because years ago you were
That Goddess whose blood
Adorned the sacred stream.
Dances and glances
In cries and laughter,
In flowing tears.
Motionless I observe you
As you flaunt with the dance
Of your sacred body
The laughter and tears
You repress for me.

Llantos y risas

Mis ojos buscan
Lo que tu cuerpo entrega,
Cuando entre pasos y golpes
Expresas en ti
La danza de ancestros enjutos.
Miro y escucho
Lo que tu cuerpo canta,
Cuando entre llantos y risas
Narras en ti
La leyenda que ayer canté.
Palpo y observo
Lo que nadie ve ya en ti,
Porque antaño fuiste
Aquella diosa cuya sangre
Adornó el sacro arroyo.
Danzas y miradas
Entre gritos y risas,
Entre efluvios y lágrimas.
Yo te contemplo inerte
Mientras expresas y narras
Con tu sacro cuerpo
Los gritos y llantos
Que por mí reprimes.

Distant Loneliness

Loneliness.
I will live with it
Like all those who now live
In peace and tears.
I will suffer with it
When, today, wandering and clamoring,
I miss just one of those,
Whom I drag crying and begging,
In dark daytime solitude
That tomorrow I will share.

Loneliness with children,
Damsels in open flower,
And nights burying their shadows.
I will live with it
Like those who now live
The tears and desire they saw in me.

Today it is you, Abigael,
Because yesterday it was you
Waiting eternally alone
As I wrapped your existence with loneliness.

Tomorrow I will live with it
Because it possessed me
So that you may wait eternally alone.

Today, it is you, Abigael.
Because yesterday it was you,
And tomorrow I will live with it.

Perhaps then I will taste life,
A life infused in eternal loneliness
That only you laid bare.

Soledad lejana

Soledad.
Habré de vivir con ella
Como en ella viven
Cuantas de mí obtuvieron quietud y lágrimas.
Habré de padecer con ella
Cuando vagando y clamando,
Añore sólo una de cuantas hoy,
Envueltas en gritos y plegarias,
Arrastro en esta soledad diurna y oscura
Que mañana compartiré.

Soledad con retoños,
Doncellas en flores abiertas,
Y noches que encierran sus sombras.
Habré de vivir con ella
Como en ella viven
Cuantas en mí vivieron lágrimas y anhelo.

Hoy, eres tú, Abigael,
Porque ayer fuiste tú
Esperándome eternamente con soledad.
Mientras envolvía tu existencia con soledad.

Mañana habré de vivir con ella
Porque ella me poseyó
Para que esperaras eternamente sola.

Hoy eres tú, Abigael.
Porque ayer fuiste tú,
Y mañana habré de vivir con ella.

Quizá entonces cate la vida,
Aquella vida imbuida en la eterna soledad
Que sólo tú pregonaste.

Amalia's Secret

Vertical waters crash
Undaunted,
Into the rocks that cover our path,
The one trodden by ancestors and creatures
Searching for that first memory,
Or the coming light out of darkness.

This is our path, Amalia.
In the presence of dear ones,
Witnesses of our moist existence,
We wished to return to the memory of our first experience,
When in the water and nothingness that define us,
We search the canal defended with struggle and death.

Lower your head, Amalia,
Enter slowly,
For the opening of the crack is wise,
The big and the small pass
As through a canal.

Meanwhile, the vertical waters
Break up and down,
Singing our destiny.
We are soaked and anointed,
As we were yesterday,
Passing through the dark canal
As her master muffled her cries.

The waters crash and the rocks squeal,
And the voice in the crack strips away your secret
That turns you to cold sadness.
All is darkness, Amalia;

Inside or out, all is darkness.
Do not fall, Amalia,
Because holding on to the moist earth
Will not reveal the secret of times.
And life is the short journey
From hut-wetya to cave-böappú.
Do not grab the wet earth yet,
Because you must enter and discover
In crashing waters,
In cries and depths,
Within you is the secret, Amalia:
Your power.

El secreto de Amalia

Las aguas verticales golpean
Impías,
A las rocas que embozan el camino nuestro,
Aquel por el que transitaron ancestros y criaturas
En busca de aquel primer recuerdo,
O el paso de la oscuridad a la luz oscura.

Por él transitamos tú y yo, Amalia.
Y en presencia de allegados,
Testigos de nuestra húmeda existencia,
Quisimos regresar al recuerdo de nuestra primera experiencia,
Cuando tras la nada y el agua que nos define,
Buscamos el canal por el que luchan y mueren hombres.

Agáchate, Amalia,
Y penetra despacio,
Que la abertura de la gruta es sabia,
Porque por ella van grandes y chicos
Al igual que grandes y chicos por el canal.

Mientras tanto golpean y golpean
Desde arriba y abajo,
Las aguas verticales que cantan nuestro sino.
Estamos empapados y untados
Como lo estuvimos ayer,
Para transitar por el oscuro canal
Mientras su maestra plegaba sus gritos.

Las aguas golpean y las rocas gimen,
Y la voz de la gruta desgarra tu secreto
Que convertiste en frío y tristeza.
Todo es oscuridad, Amalia;

Dentro o fuera, todo es oscuridad.
No te caigas, Amalia,
Porque quien abraza la húmeda tierra
No entrará en el secreto de los tiempos.
Y la vida es el corto periplo
Desde la cabaña-wetya hasta la gruta-böappú.
No abraces la húmeda tierra aún,
Porque tienes que entrar y descubrir
Entre aguas y golpes,
Entre gritos y abismo,
Que llevas tu secreto en ti, Amalia:
Tu poder.

Woman of the Valley

In the Olympus of the Goddesses
She lives in song.
The beauty Wewèöbwáró;
Also walking in the high valleys
The damsels who lost their flower
In the red lagoon of the vintner Si´ema.

And I sing the romance of Wewèöbwáró
As the agile vintner
Carefully prunes and harvests:
" ´N ké si´ema köpé köpé
Ë se sí öbwása mavíla máó
La malobé,
Nyíbela ólo ríë ölló tywé re
Össó tó së mëeká . . . "9

The Damsels of Wewèöbwáró wander,
In silence,
Over the high valley of the king-guide Möókáta;
And the goddesses anxiously await
The woman of our olympic valley,
Yesterday young and virginal,
Today solitary damsel of open flower.

Old Si´ema no longer climbs,
And Wewèöbwáró has left the high valley;

9. There the valiant vintner
Who will bloody our palm trees,
Letting the tender date fall to eat it
And the bunch to extract the seeds . . .

Who will tell of the gentlemen?
Who will unsettle the quiet existence
Of ancestors and weeping mothers?

Sleep, Si´ema;
Rest peacefully while
She irrigates the valley with those red waters
That her damsels left behind no longer searching
For the men, the vintners.

La mujer del valle

En el olimpo de las diosas
Mora en canto,
La bella Wewèöbwáró;
Y en el alto valle transitan
Aquellas doncellas que dejaron su flor
En las rojas aguas de la poza de Si´ema (vinatero).

Y yo canto la romanza de Wewèöbwáró
Mientras el vinatero ágil
Poda con recodo y desgarra racimos:
"´N ké si´ema köpé köpé
Ë se sí öbwása mavíla máó
La malobé,
Nyíbela ólo ríë ölló tywé re
Össó tó së mëeká . . ."[10]

Las doncellas de Wewèöbwáró vagan,
Calladas,
Por el alto valle del rey-guía Möókáta;
Y las diosas guardan celosas
A la mujer del valle del olimpo nuestro,
Ayer joven doncella en flor,
Hoy solitaria doncella de flor abierta.

Ya no trepa el anciano Si´ema,
Y Wewèöbwáró dejó ya el valle alto;

---

10. He ahí el valiente vinatero
El que sangrará nuestras palmeras,
Deja caer el tierno dátil para comerlo
Y el racimo para romper las semillas . . .

¿Quién hablará a los donceles?
¿Quién violará la quieta existencia
De ancestros y madres en llanto?

Duerme, Si´ema;
Vela quietamente mientras
Ella riega el valle con aquellas rojas aguas
Que sus doncellas dejaron en busca, tardíamente,
De cuantos hombres fueron vinateros.

Muted Cries

They say you were exiled long ago
And that today you live in still waters,
Yesterday the place of vintners in gonads.

They say you are all those who arrived today,
Because you told of all of them in legends
Leaving no trace or form.

Today I contemplate, calmly.
The print blurred by red waters.
Today I listen, thinking
The deep song of still waters.

Which one is your face?
Which one is my face?

They say I am of the seven powers
But which ones?
And they say all are in you,
Because you are woman,
Because my dwelling is in you.

Gritos enmudecidos

Dicen que fuiste desterrada antaño
Y que hoy vives en las quietas aguas,
Ayer lugar de vinateros en gónadas.

Dicen que eras todas las que hoy llegaron,
Porque de todas hablaste en leyendas
Sin dejar ni rostro ni forma.

Hoy contemplo, callado,
La impronta que robaron las rojas aguas.

Hoy escucho, pensando,
El canto hondo de las quietas aguas.

¿Cuál es tu rostro?
¿Cuál es mi rostro?

Dicen que soy de los siete poderes
Mas ignoro cuáles son éstos,
Y dicen que todos están en ti,
Porque eres mujer,
Y porque en ti está mi morada.

Furtive Verses

The black women's dance to the beat of the bell chimes and maracas invites the dancing Gods to dwell in the elders who leap, unstoppable, mindless of their age, arching their bodies with short rapid jumps;

It is the dance of the shady nubile young women who anoint their bodies with oil and the sweat of their still tender skin, a potion evoking their blood as in the old times when it colored the crystalline waters of the River Eölá, waters that I drank downstream and whose spell I am under and always will be;

It is the dance of desperate and cadaverous gentlemen who search the coveted, sacred, pompous, vibrating breasts, where they shall rest their tired and hoary heads; recalling what they were, their hidden origin and limited life.

It is the dancing song of becoming old and of puberty extending its virginity, its tender coveted flower:

Where are you, black water?

Where is the waving arm that leads me to the dark world, to assure me that none of what I see–breasts, bottocks–is real?

Versos furtivos

Es el baile de las negras jóvenes al son de los golpes de la campana y la maraca que invitan a los Dioses danzantes a morar en los ancianos que saltan imparables y desprecian los pesados años, arqueando sus figuras con saltos cortos y rápidos;

Es el baile de las oscuras jóvenes casaderas que untan su cuerpo con toola y el sudor que emana de su todavía tierna piel, pócima que recuerda aquella sangre suya con la que tiñeron una vez las cristalinas aguas del río Eölá, aguas que yo bebí más abajo y cuyo hechizo llevo dentro y siempre;

Es el baile de los desesperados y enjutos donceles que buscan los anhelados, codiciados, sacros y pomposos pechos que retiemblan, y sobre los que habrán de reclinar su cansada y ya canosa cabeza; recordando lo que fueron y hasta su propio origen oculto y embelesada vida.

Es el canto de la vejez que baila y de la pubertad que extiende virgen su tierna flor codiciada:

¿Dónde estás, agua negra?

¿Dónde está el brazo que me conduce al oscuro mundo, para recordarme que nada de lo que veo, pechos o nalgas, es cierto?

Memories

Today I wish to think I am a memory,
Maybe it's my desperate will
To store those desired moments.
Today I want to think
You are a distant memory,
A dream dreamed long ago
As the waves crash
Under the shine of a shy moon.

I want to think that still you are arriving
And that you will knock on my door
Lightly,
And I shall let you in, slowly,
And, discreetly, stealthily you will enter.

Today I wish to say:
"He will not be here at night
When the fast falling star awakens me,
When desperately I want him in me.
He will not be here when his skin
Is buried in the darkness of moonlight."

Today I wish to think him closer
Because he is far,
Because I have only the memory
Hidden by the night.
Today I wish to believe he is not here
Although I think it a memory
Returning,
A blurry memory
Between dream and life,
Between tears and muffled sobs.

Recuerdos

Hoy quiero pensar que soy un recuerdo,
Quizá para guardar ansiosa
Los momentos que tanto deseo.
Hoy quiero pensar
Que eres un recuerdo lejano,
Un deseo soñado antaño
Entre los golpes de las olas
Y la luz de una tímida luna.

Quiero pensar que todavía vas llegando
Y que llamarás a mi puerta
Con suaves golpes,
Y que yo abriré, despacio,
Para que entres discreto, furtivo.

Hoy quiero pensar:
"No estará cuando de noche
Me desvele la luz de una fugaz estrella,
Cuando le desee desesperada en mí.
No estará cuando su piel se ahogue
En la oscura noche que la luna ilumina."

Hoy quiero pensar que está más cerca
Porque no está,
Porque sólo me queda el recuerdo
Que la noche oculta.
Hoy quiero pensar que no está
Aunque piense que es un recuerdo
Que empieza a volver de nuevo,
Un recuerdo confuso
Entre sueño y vida,
Entre lágrimas y llantos plegados.

Snail and Snake

I live calmly waiting
Between blows and drops
A fresh warm sweat
Oozing from your dark skin.
I listen and confirm
The smothered cries that shape
Calmly,
Your dark hidden lips.
I enter and wait
And exit quickly when
Bangs sound in the sacred lagoon.
I endure and you endure
As I come and go;
Sheathe it! you say
Meanwhile,
I come and go fast
Searching that hidden embrace
Between snake and snail.

Caracol y serpiente

Vivo y aguardo calmo

Entre golpe y gotas

El fresco y cálido sudor

Que emana de tu oscura piel.

Escucho y reclamo

Los sofocados gritos que moldean

Calmos,

Tus oscuros y ocultos labios.

Entro y aguardo

Y salgo presto cuando

Los golpes se anuncian en la poza sacra.

Aguanto y aguantas

Mientras entro y salgo;

¡Envaina! Dices

Y mientras,

Entro y salgo presto

Buscando aquel abrazo oculto

Entre la serpiente y el caracol.

Sudden Desire

"If you leave me tomorrow,

With my dark eyes I will follow,

Motionless,

Watching you fade

Step by step,

Although I desire your black shadow

In the dark and clear and harsh sundown.

And I will remember that first break

Caused by your innocent stare;

But I will not tell you to return,

And if you do,

I will be the wounded woman

Still feeling

That first hurt;

Not even time could heal it.

Love me quickly now

Because I loved you slowly,

And do not stop:

Blood exposes the pain, the tears."

Presto deseo

"Si mañana me dejas,
Te seguiré con mis oscuros ojos
Quieta,
Viendo cómo te alejas
Paso a paso,
Aunque añore tu negra sombra
De tardes oscuras y blancas y ácidas.
Y recordaré aquella primera brecha
Causada por tu inocente mirada;
Pero no diré que vuelvas,
Y si lo haces
Encontrarás en mí a la mujer herida
Que todavía siente
Aquel primer dolor
Que ni el tiempo logra enterrar.
Ámame presto ahora
Porque yo te amé lentamente,
Pero no envaines:
La sangre anuncia dolor y llanto."

Voices

Voices.

Distant voices in the breeze;

Round shadows hear them

From the clear bottom;

Voices in the beat

And sound of a tired throat,

Voices you feel and follow

With your tired and curved body.

Who will sound them tomorrow,

When that tired throat is broken,

Or when your back is hunched?

Who will cry out your glory,

Young Black woman of sweat and clay?

Who will nurse from those split wet breasts

Before they wilt forever

Who will extend a hand,

Now and always, searching

In the water for your worn skin

Tracing your entire body?

Who?

Now,

The voices you hear and follow will be,

Tomorrow,

The distant voices floating in the quiet breeze.

Voces

Voces.

Lejanas voces llevadas por el viento calmo

Que las arqueadas sombras escuchan

Desde el fondo claro,

Voces que funden el ritmo

Y el son que nace de la garganta cansada,

Voces que sientes y marcas

Con tu cansado y arqueado cuerpo.

¿Quién las hará mañana,

Cuando se rompa la garganta cansada,

O cuando camines enjuta?

¿Quién gritará tu gloria,

Joven de negra piel y sudor y barro?

¿Quién beberá de tus húmedos pechos partidos

Antes de enlaciarse para siempre?

¿Quién tenderá la mano para buscar,

Ahora y siempre

Tu piel entre el agua arcillada

Que por tu cuerpo corre?

¿Quién?

Ahora,

Las voces que sientes y maras serán,

Mañana,

Las lejanas voces llevadas por el viento calmo.

Rátyííla la Bö (Twenty and Ten)

What are twenty and ten
If not late afternoon falling
And time dying
Or a cold breeze
Of the woman and man,
You and me?
What can twenty and ten be
If not the fire we stoke
Or the hut we build,
Or the yams we cultivate
For the little one of our future
When the old lady returns?
What are twenty and ten
If not the amount I miss you
The day that is
And was not,
Or the groom
Of the bride
When I speak and you listen,
When you yell and I am silent,
When I advance and regress
When you search and I find.
What are twenty and ten?

Rátyííla la Bö (Veinte y diez)

¿Qué son veinte y diez
Sino la tarde que cae
Y el tiempo que muere,
O la brisa gélida
De la mujer y hombre que somos
Tú y yo?
¿Qué son veinte y diez
Sino el fuego que avivamos
Y la choza que levantamos,
O el ñamal que cuidamos
Para ese retoño que llega
De ese alguien que es
Cuando regresa la anciana?
¿Qué son veinte y diez
Sino yo que te extraño
En un día que es
Y no fue,
O el hombre consorte
De la esposa que casa
Cuando hablo y escuchas,
Cuando gritas y callo,
Cuando avanzo y reculo,
Cuando buscas y hallo.
¿Qué son veinte y diez?

Furtive Lover

Again I will contemplate your dark skin,
My gaze will become the waters caressing you;
I will sing your name as drops
Fall on your face from above,
Those coveted waters
That today caress your dark skin.

I will hide in the wild grass
And I will endure the falling water,
Irrigating our solitary path.

Again I will contemplate your dark skin
And I will want to fight the water
That hides your worn skin.
I will arrive at your dwelling before you
And I will light the fire,
The warmth you refused yesteryear.
And I will be the eyes that watch you
As you stoke the fire,
The ears that hear
Your sad melodic notes,
And the arms that receive
You, straight or thin,
As you dream that old dream
With the joyous life you no longer tell.

Amante furtivo

Volveré a contemplar tu oscura piel,
Confundiré mi mirada con el brillo
De las aguas que te acarician;
Cantaré tu nombre mientras las gotas
Golpean desde arriba tu faz,
Aquellas aguas que envidio
Y que hoy acarician tu oscura piel.

Me ocultaré entre la crecida maleza
Y resistiré entre los golpes del agua que cae,
Agua que regará nuestra solitaria senda.

Volveré a contemplar tu oscura piel
Y desearé luchar contra el agua
Que confunde tu cuerpo arcilloso.
Llegaré antes a tu morada
Y encenderé el fuego y calor
Que antaño negaste.
Y seré los ojos que te vean
Mientras avivas tu fuego,
Los oídos que escuchen
Tus tristes y cortas melodías,
Y los brazos que te reciban
Cuando erguida o enjuta,
Sueñes que soñaste alguna vez
Con la dichosa vida que ahora callas.

Dancing and Shouting

Shake,

Shout and jump,

Dance and shout.

Dance, make your free breasts shiver,

Move the center between your legs

And allow me the ecstasy of loving your darkness.

Dance and mark

The reflection of an absent light,

The song of a shine unseen.

Feel it and shout it and shake it

But dance

Dance when I uncover your new skin,

Hidden in the heat of the night

And the chasm of the dancing thighs

In the woman of the misty body.

Gritos y danzas

Tiembla,

Grita y salta,

Pero baila.

Baila porque tiemblen tus desviados pechos,

Mueve tus crecidas vulvas

Y deja que en éxtasis ame tu oscura belleza.

Baila y muestra

El reflejo de la luz ausente,

Canto del silencio negro

Y piel que brilla oculta.

Siente y tiembla y grita

Pero baila,

Baila cuando descubra tu conversa piel,

Oculta en el calor de la noche

Y abismo de las nalgas que bailan

En la mujer de nalgas y cuerpo en bruma.

Wrinkled Rocks

And I found naked rocks

As myriad conches gathered in my hand;

And I discovered my flow in your skin

In the fog and the groans

Today dreaming of my fleeting presence.

Rocks bathed by crashes

As my boats plough through the turbulent waters

Searching the destiny of old.

And I shall embrace the waters

In the foam's white shadows

That hide the surrendered rocks

In your clothes and mine.

And I will search your shadow in the fog

When embraces sculpted you in the night

As the rough waters flowed

In silent songs and cries.

Rocas arcilladas

Y encontré las rocas desnudas
Mientras en mi palma moraban conchas menudas;
Y confundí mi efluvio en tu piel
Entre niebla y gemidos
Soñando hoy con mi fugaz estancia.
Rocas bañadas entre golpes
Mientras surcan mis bravas aguas mis barcas
Buscando el sino de antaño.
Y abrazaré las aguas
Entre las blancas sombras
Que ocultan las poseídas rocas
Entre prenda y prenda.
Y buscaré tu sombra en la niebla
Cuando en abrazos fuiste esculpida en la noche
Mientras fluía el agua brava
Entre cantos y gritos callados.

Furtive Tears

The moon will shine like soft fire,
And your tender dark skin
Will be its night dwelling;
I will count my white hairs in your hands
In the midst of chirping crickets,
In the flight of a furtive star.
I will sing softly as you embrace the night,
And like a wounded warrior
Still clasping his lance,
I will await the sad end
Of the last fire
That you will grasp in the cavernous night.
And because all is open,
My song will be possessed;
And in the howling salvos
Bewitching the night
You will lie fearless,
As you recall a time that wished to be;
When I wandered possessed inside you.
And because I blur nothing,
My song will be exposed
And in your slow supplications;
I will receive the light born of your eyes;
And you will exist,
Because in you I will find
And in you I will possess,
And in you will be my Goddess Bisila.

Lágrimas furtivas

El fuego tenue de la luna lucirá,
Y tu tierna y oscura piel
Será su morada en la noche viva;
Contaré mis canas en tus manos
Entre el canto del grillo
Y el viaje de la estrella furtiva.
Cantaré plegado mientras abrazas la noche,
Y cuan guerrero herido
Y agarrado a su lanza,
Esperaré infausto
La venida del último fuego
Que abrazarás en la noche cavernal.
Y porque nada se oculta,
Mi canto será poseído;
Y en las salvas aullantes
Que embelesan la noche
Yacerás tendida y brava,
Mientras recuerdas el tiempo que quiso ser,
Cuando erraba y fui en ti posado.
Y porque nada enturbio,
Mi canto será prensado,
Y en tus lentas plegarias
Recibiré la luz que de tus ojos nace;
Y serás,
Porque en ti hallaré
Y en ti poseeré,
Y en ti será mi Diosa Bisila.

Echo and Chaos

Missed drops in lakes and valleys;
Dark is the path I walk alone
In hard rain
And clamoring tearful souls.

I go because I never returned
And I came because I never arrived,
Because my harp thundered in the darkness
When yesterday you were transported
By Gods and Gentlemen and Ancestors.

Today my hunched body walks,
Looking for your gift;
Today motionless and calm, I implore good fortune,
As I await silently
The flight of my unscathed soul.

My God came and placed me on you,
My life solidly at your side,
And my spirit illuminated our destiny:
I lie here before you, transparent,
After the fall of the day.
I am of you because I was not,
And for you I desire because I did not possess:
I present myself to you, my Goddess-Mother.

Eco y caos

Golpes inciertos en charcas y valles:
Oscuro el camino que recorro ajeno
Entre lluvias que abrasan
Y almas que claman en lágrimas vivas.

Voy porque nunca volví
Y vine porque jamás llegué,
Porque mi arpa tronó entre nieblas
Cuando ayer fuiste portada
Por Dioses y Donceles y Ancestros.

Hoy camino enjuto,
Buscando hallar aquello que de ti recibí;
Hoy imploro mi fortuna, quieto y calmo,
Mientras espero callado
El vuelo de mi alma incólume.

Mi Dios vino y me posó en ti,
Y mi vida se fundió a tu vera,
Y mis celos alumbraron nuestro sino:
Heme ante ti yacer, límpido,
Ya caído el día.
De ti soy porque no fui
Y por ti anhelo porque no poseí:
Heme ante ti, mi Diosa-Madre.

Waters and Moon

And Moon descended to clear Waters
Moistening your body with fog and fire
In words and fireflies at rest.

And Moon faced your eyes
Cupping Water from them painlessly
And raining directly on me.

Water and Moon compete for your body,
Glowing in the darkness.

But night has fallen
And like a cricket I sing my song,
Because Waters and Moon do not see
When I enter you.

You are and will be my witness, Moon,
When I remember tomorrow,
In fog and flow,
The body you moistened
With your light and clear Waters.

Aguas y Luna

Y la Luna bajó a las Aguas claras
Rociando tu cuerpo en nieblas y fuego
Entre palabras y luciérnagas quietas.

Y la luna se posó en tus ojos
Cogiendo de ellos el Agua que sin dolor
Me llueve y reclama.

Agua y Luna disputan tu cuerpo
Entre reflejos y tinieblas.

Pero ya es de noche
Y cuan grillo inicio mi canto,
Porque ni Aguas ni Luna perciben
Cuándo me adentro en ti.

Eres y serás mi testigo, Luna,
Cuando recuerde mañana,
Entre nieblas y efluvios,
A aquel cuerpo que rociaste
Con tu luz y las Aguas claras.

Eyes and Logs

Today I saw eyes yours and not yours.
Because in them flashed
A fire I stoked in the cold drizzling afternoons
When I returned weary and drenched.

These are the eyes of fire
That cover the soft log
Slowly and cruelly growing smaller.

I saw the sweet and cold fire
With its dark grey flames
As your eyes shone in its glow,
Unknown, without a clear color,
Only the flames emerging from the high earth
Lancing its entrails here and there.

It is your eyes that see for me,
It is your fire eyes
The volcano color:
Eyes of wood, yours,
Eyes of fire and volcano,
Eyes that will see for me.

Ojos y leños

Hoy he visto ojos que son y no son tuyos.
Porque antes brotó en ellos
El fuego que avivé en las frías tardes lluviosas
Cuando volvía cansado ya aguado.

Son los ojos de fuego
Que cubren el tierno leño
Consumido lenta y cruelmente.

Con sus llamas oscuras y grises
Vi el fuego dulce y frío
Mientras tus ojos brillaban en su luz,
Sin color sabido ni visto
Salvo del fuego que brota de la tierra alta
Y lanza sus entrañas acá y allá.

Son tus ojos los que ven por mí.
Son tus ojos de fuego
En su color de volcán:
Ojos de leño y tuyos,
Ojos de fuego y volcán,
Ojos que verán por mí.

The Final Step

Women walk and search
When night arrives in their dwellings,
Laughing and weaving gazes and furtive cries
As they tie their knots with sweat and tears.

Blessed is he who finds in the convert's psalms
The remains of women who walk and seek
As they step in puddles and ponds.

This the summary of my destiny
I offer in absent cries awaiting silently:

Gazing, seeing, possessed and drenched in tears.

El paso final

Ellas caminan y buscan
Cuando la noche acude a sus moradas,
Ríen y tejen miradas y llantos furtivos
Mientras estrechan sus lazos con sudor y sangre.

Dichoso aquel que halla en salmos conversos
Los restos de aquellas que caminan y buscan
Mientras andan en charcas y pozas.

Así se resume mi sino
En llantos ausentes mientras guardo y callo:

Mirando, viendo, poseído y llorado.

The Sentence

Execute them, execute them
Strip the life out of them,
Let their still warm blood flow
And let it fertilize the earth!

Do it now,
For they no longer have ears
And they cannot dance like "böatte";
They can no longer ring their "bilëbbó" bells
When tomorrow dancing in silence
To the quiet beat of the ancestors,
For today their tongues are split
Their eyes gouged
And their gonads singed.

Strip them of life
And spill their blood in the lake
So that Wewèöpö can look for them
To cease their damsels' lament.

Elders and young gentlemen,
Naked and clothed,
No one remembers them
Only the blood fertilizing the earth
With the word liberty;
The blood of elders and young men
The blood of a people with earth from the sea
The blood of liberty and words.

La sentencia

¡Fusiladles, fusiladles
Quitadles la vida,
Derramad su sangre aún cálida
Para que brote de la húmeda tierra!

Hacedlo ahora,
Porque ya no tienen orejas
Ni pueden dar los pasos del "böatte";
Ya no podrán sujetar los "bilëbbó"
Cuando mañana asistan callados,
Al baile quieto de los ancestros,
Porque hoy tienen la lengua partida
Los ojos reventados
Y sus gónadas chamuscadas.

Quitadles la vida
Y derramad su sangre en el lago
Para que Wewèöpö les busque
Y cesen los lamentos de sus doncellas.

Viejos y donceles,
Desnudos o cubiertos,
Ya nadie les recuerda
Sólo la sangre que fecundó la tierra
Y de la que germinó y siempre
La palabra libertad;
La sangre de ancianos y donceles
La sangre de un pueblo con tierra de mar
La sangre de la libertad y la lengua.

The Date

Night in repose
As I sit surrounded by you
Under watchful stars
Shining wildly on your body possessed
In the clear cold night:
Dark time in fog and water.
In the midst of moans and fire
Moving on your still body,
Once possessed in water and moon,
In hills and trails,
Gentle bites
As you adorn my mind with loud struggling desire.
I take the tempo down
I lengthen my song,
With my weapon
I stab a stare at others staring.
Tomorrow you will be the Flower
Exalted in thrones and lights,
Ivory white damsel
Still in red Flowers
Harmonizing my song in memories.
Joy and fortune define your soul
As I embrace you as before
Born of tears,
You lie confused, absorbed,
Gently cooing,
Deeds folded in laments and fog
Hidden in the clear night.

La cita

La noche reposa
Mientras descanso tapiado en ti
Ante los testigos de las estrellas
Rayadas por la luz que brota
Indómita de tu cuerpo poseído
En la noche clara:
Tiempo oscuro
Entre niebla y agua.
Entre gemidos y fuego
Sobre tu cuerpo quieto,
Poseído otrora entre aguas y luna,
Entre montes y sendas,
Ronchando mientras
Ornas mi mente en gritos y lid.
Adagio mi danza,
Largo mi canto,
Adarga llevo cuando
Sello miradas otras.
Serás mañana la Flor
Injerta en tronos y luces,
Ebúrnea doncella clara
Todavía en Flores rojas
Entonando entre recuerdos mi canto.
Sentido y dicha definen tu alma
Ante abrazos contados
Naciendo de lágrimas mientras
Yazgas confusa y absorta,
Arrullando quieta,
Gesta plegada entre gemidos y niebla
Oculta en la clara noche.

Epilogue

I should say it, but not to boast or smile at the generosity or cruelty of the reader or critic: I was never a poet, and I will never claim that status, that is, unless I search for the meaning of my journey through the language of my haphazard oppressor, an actor playing the role of someone engulfed in pain as I lay bare everything my ancestors were but I could not be.

With these verses, on target or not, I calmly wish to reflect the details of a culture I cling to in order to be what I do not remember. This is why I seek ancestors in legends, damsels, the young men and the happenings of time ago, and I search furtively those very beings in my own vulnerable existence.

I want to fill gaps; this is why I submerge myself my inner emptiness, so that I can populate my world with Wewèöpö, Ùri, Löbëla, Bula wÉsa´a, Möhókó, etc., with my own reality, a world of beings that you, I, all of us, manipulate.

And we are language, and language is the world of what we see, saw, and will see, no matter who we are: Bubi or Spanish.

Ntá-Bösöpé Bölëkia B.

Epílogo

Bueno es decirlo. Y lo diré no para jactarme ni sonreír tras la benevolencia o crueldad del lector y crítico. Nunca fue ni será mi propósito presentarme como poeta porque no lo soy ni lo seré, al menos mientras busque en los versos el sentido de mi duro periplo que hoy pretendo apuntalar con la lengua de mi incurioso opresor, actor de cuanto dolor me engulle, al desgarrar de mí todo cuanto fueron mis ancestros y que no pude ser.

Con estos versos, acertados o no, indago quieto en busca del menor reflejo cultural al que aferrarme para ser lo que no recuerdo. Por eso busco ancestros en leyendas, doncellas y donceles, en hechos acaecidos ayer, para luego, y furtivamente, encontrar tales seres en mi indefensa existencia.

Quiero colmar mis carencias, por eso me sumerjo en mi vacuidad interior para poblar mi mundo con las realidades que vivo con Wewèöpö, Úri, Löbëla, Bula wÉsa´á, Möhókó, etc., un mundo de seres manipulados por ti, por mí, por nosotros.

Y nosotros somos la lengua, y la lengua es el mundo de cuanto vemos, vimos o veremos, sea bubi o española.

Ntá-Bösöpé Bölëkia B.

The Damsels of Old

Who was Wewèöpö?
Who was Wésëpa?
Who engendered Bula wÉsa´á?
Who sang to Úri?
Who possessed Löbëla?
Who narrated Möhókó?

They were all cut into caves
For seven moons
Leading to doors to the ancestral world
Where the gods of the seven powers dwell.

A power for each one
For each one is a woman.
Fair Wewèöpö is valor,
Wésëpa incarnates cautious pride,
Bula wÉsa´á is innocent strength,
Úri refinement and abnegation,
Löbëla the happiness bestowed to the lover
And Möhókó the gleaming tear.

All, damsels and absent mothers,
Were protected by mother Börihí,
And all went in search for si´ema,
Who years ago ploughed through seas and caverns.

All left and all stayed,
All returned and no one left when
Under destiny's waters
Dwelled the warriors Baekka,
All loved by Ebi´ò ö Wáasa
And none possessed by him.
I do not hold grudges nor do I talk of happiness
Nor do I talk of glories or disasters.
I only contemplate, still and absent,
The damsels who surround my dwelling,
Among goddesses and cave dwellers
Tomorrow water and nothing.

Las doncellas de antaño

¿Quién fue Wewèöpö?
¿Quién vio a Wésëpa?
¿Quién engendró a Bula wÉsa´á?
¿Quién cantó a Úri?
¿Quién poseyó a Löbëla?
¿Quién narró a Möhókó?

Todas fueron troqueladas en grutas
Durante siete lunas,
A las puertas que llevan al mundo ancestral
Donde moran los dioses de los siete poderes.

Un poder para cada una,
Porque cada una es mujer.
Wewèöpö es la bella osadía,
Wésëpa encarna el orgullo prudente,
Bula wÉsa´á es la fuerza inocente,
Úri la delicadeza y abnegación,
Löbëla la dicha que otorga al amado
Y Möhókó, la lágrima reluciente.

Todas ellas, doncellas y madres ausentes,
Fueron veladas por la madre Börihí,
Y todas fueron en busca del doncel si´ema
Que antaño surcó mares y grutas.

Todas fueron y todas quedaron,
Todas volvieron y ninguna fue cuando,
Bajo las aguas del destino,
Moraron los guerreros baekka,
Todas fueron amadas por Ebi´ò ö Wáasa
Y ninguna fue por él poseída.
No albergo ni dichas ni penurias
Tampoco narro glorias ni desastres.
Sólo contemplo, quieto y ausente,
A las doncellas que circundan mi morada,
Entre diosas y habitantes grutales
Que hogaño serán aguas y nada.

A Look Inside

Where the triumph and trumpet
When your body lies fetal
When you don't see and don't look,
And you don't feel
And you don't live?

Today I hear and see,
Because I need and hope.

Today I look and see,
Because I desire and don't taste.

The languid light of day falls
And grey night approaches,
Like the tired and decrepit life
That brings on the quiet sleep
Of those men and women,
Present beings,
Who were here yesterday,
They were what others desired.

Today I cover myself with fog and silence,
Silent, no glory, nothing,
Because this is how I arrived, empty,
And this is how I will leave, empty,
With only the memory of those left,
Like you, interring my quick destiny.

Today I cover myself with water and earth,
Voiceless, silent, nothing,
As you listen and perceive
The tired voices advancing my quiet sleep,
A path traveled by those whose children and elders,
Were yesterday anointed in cracks and vulvas.

Where the glory and pomp
When I rest furiously alone
And look and don't see,
And when I am and don't feel and don't live?

Mirada adentro

¿Dónde quedará el ruido y la gloria cuando
Postrado con recodo y quieto,
No veas ni mires,
Ni vivas ni sientas?

Hoy escucho y percibo,
Porque quiero y anhelo.

Hoy miro y veo,
Porque deseo y no cato.

La luz lánguida del día cae
Y avanza la noche gris,
Como la cansada y decrépita vida
Que avanza el sueño quieto
De aquellos y aquellas que ayer,
Seres en presencia,
Fueron lo que otros quisieron y desearon.

Hoy me cubro entre nieblas y silencio,
Sin ruido, sin gloria, sin nada,
Porque así vine, vacío,
Y así me retiro, vacío,
Con el solo recuerdo de quienes como tú,
Quedan enterrando mi fugaz destino.

Hoy me cubro entre aguas y tierra,
Sin ruido, sin voz, sin nada,
Mientras escuchas y percibes
Las voces que cansadas avanzaron mi sueño quieto,
Camino que transitaban quienes,
Niños o ancianos,
Ayer fueron ungidos en grutas y vulvas.

¿Dónde quedará el ruido y la gloria cuando,
Tendido con furia y parco,
Mire y no vea,
Sea y no sienta ni viva?

Sunken Eyes

My eyes are your eyes
And I face what your eyes don't want to see:
Wrinkled faces and sunken eyes
Among haughty bodies in the mist.

Your eyes are my eyes
And I see what my eyes wish not to see:
Men with broken and empty gonads
Among long breasts of women gazing absently.

My eyes are my eyes
And your eyes are my eyes,
Because you will see what I wish not to see,
Or shall see what I could not see;
When the strong fragrance of men and women
Embraces and sucks me in.

Only the children
Tell of those who today
Expose their wrinkled faces and sunken eyes
In the midst of gazes and stench
In the midst of their hazy bodies in the midst.

Ojos hundidos

Mis ojos son tus ojos
Y miro lo que tus ojos quieren no ver:
Rostros disecados y ojos hundidos
Entre cuerpos fatuos en la bruma.

Tus ojos son mis ojos
Y veo lo que mis ojos quieren no mirar:
Hombres de gónadas estiradas y vacías
Entre largos senos de mujeres con miradas ausentes.

Mis ojos son mis ojos
Y tus ojos son mis ojos,
Porque tú verás lo que no quiero ver,
O verás lo que no pude ver,
Cuando la fuerte fragancia de hombres y mujeres
Me abrace y sea en ella imbuido.

Sólo los retoños cuentan
Qué fue de aquellos que hoy exponen
Entre miradas y hedores,
Rostros disecados y ojos hundidos
En sus cuerpos confusos en la bruma.

Love?

Shut up,
Don't speak!
Words:
Just death and laughter.
Shut up today!
Don't talk now.
Tomorrow will come.
And love?
Shut up today!
Because it will come tomorrow
And I am of today.

¿Amor?

¡Cállate,
No hables!
Las palabras:
Sólo muerte y risas.
¡Cállate hoy!
Y no hables ahora.
Mañana vendrá.
¿Y el amor?
¡Cállate hoy!
Porque vendrá mañana
Y yo soy de hoy.

Thoughts From the Translator

"Listen to history in verse narrated from the archives of our idyllic Bubi community, the life of yesterday and tomorrow, with moaning furtive beings as guests" (*Löbëla*, "Muffled Cries").[1] This is what Justo Bolekia Boleká (b. 1954) wants us to do as readers: listen. Although the tone of the "Introduction" to his collection of poetry suggests that we non-Bubis will not have a clue as to the meaning of his poems, the verses themselves, their spirit, their invocations, their recreations of a real-imaginary world, of a fused past-future-present, all belie the author's (pretended) skepticism. For we English speakers (Spanish readers as well) are Bolekia's "other." He has made it clear that the ideal receptor of his message is Bubi (those he would call his own) (*Löbëla*, "Introduction"), yet at the same time I sense there are many instances in these verses when the poet, while never loosing sight of his specific milieu, goes well beyond it. Like any poet worth reading and declaiming, he makes a bold gesture toward the universal. This, I think is an act of a generous spirit: it is his hope that the non-Bubi reader can also see him-herself in these images.

Indeed, the knowledge of the ethnicity and the complex historical circumstances surrounding it are crucial. The information is at times difficult to get hold of, especially if you are not a reader of Spanish. However it is out there for inquiring minds. Essentially, and forgive the simplification, the Bubis are an ethnic group predominantly from Equatorial Guinea on the island of Bioko, formerly Fernando Poo, although they also reside in other countries of central western Africa such as Nigeria, Cameroon, and Gabon. Equatorial Guinea, the broader context out of which these verses flow, is perhaps a good point of departure for those unfamiliar with this area of the globe. It is a country of a little over half a million inhabitants not including those living outside its present geographical boundaries, many in Spain due to the former colonial relationship between the two nations. In terms of land mass, it consists of several islands, the main one being Bioko (capital Malabo) in the Gulf of Guinea. Also influential in the Equatorial Guinean diaspora is the history of post colonial political repression.

---

1. The Spanish text I have been working with is *Löbëla* (Madrid: Casa de Africa, Sial, 1999), edited by Basilio Rodríguez who has kindly allowed me to translate the collection.

Thoughts From the Translator

To the southeast of Bioko is a larger continental area called Rio Muni bordered by Cameroon on the north and Gabon on the south. Perhaps one of the most frequently cited facts about Equatorial Guinea is that it is the only country in Africa south of the Sahara where Spanish is an official language. As a matter of fact one could say that Spanish is the lingua franca; most, if not all Equatorial Guineans speak it, it is the language taught in schools and the language of governmental records. However, there are several other languages spoken in the area: Fang, Bubi, Ndowe (or Benga), Anabonese, and Pichin, or Pidgin English. The citizens of the colony sought and achieved independence from Spain in 1968, a year relatively late in terms of the independence of African countries–the first countries to acquire independence did so in the 1950s. But the political and social patterns of the post-independence of Equatorial Guinea are familiar to those of us interested in African history. The end of colonial rule was followed by a brutal dictatorship lasting a decade under Francisco Macías, and autocratic rule has continued since then under Macías's nephew, Teodoro Obiang who successfully plotted a coup and quickly executed his uncle in 1979 while making no significant changes in the oligarchical political system, a government in which, according to Amnesty International, the ruling group under Obiang imprison political dissidents, often torture or execute them, and perpetuate a major income gap that keeps most of the citizens impoverished with absence of potable water and frequent failures in electricity, while the rulers live in luxury with bank accounts in foreign lands.[2] The culprit in all this is not only the dictator and his clan of sycophants, it is the oil boom. Equatorial Guinea happens to be one of the richest countries in the world in oil deposits, both on and off shore. Indeed, as many, such as Robert Klitgaard (*Tropical Gangsters*) have said, oil has kept Mr. Obiang in power.

Bolekia has written not only about Equatorial Guinea but about his ethnic group, the Bubis. In fact one of his major accomplishments as an academic—a professor of linguistics and French Philology at the University of Salamanca–is the compilation of a dictionary of the Bubi language, a work he has completed basically on his own, the first to attempt to normalize that language, something like what Antonio de Nebrija did for Spanish in 1492. In this work and in many others Bolekia shows us a spirit of defiance,

---

2. "Money Laundering and Foreign Corruption: Enforcement and Effectiveness of the Patriot Act. A Case Study Involving Riggs Bank." United States Senate Permanent Subcommittee on Investigations (2004). http://hsgac.senate.gov/index.cfm?Fuseaction=Documents.Home&FileType_id=2.

Thoughts From the Translator

for to create single-handedly a dictionary of a language on the verge of extinction is an act of resistance. This predisposition to resist oppression and unjustified authority is something his own ethnic group is known for historically—thus the many references in his poetry to warriors and their once heroic deeds. In the 1920s, the Bubis gave the Spanish colonizers a hard time, so much so that the Spanish preferred to deal with other groups less combative, more compliant. And in later years, as Equatorial Guinea became independent thus prompting a vicious dictatorship from within, many Bubis and many Equatorial Guineans of other ethnicities paid for their resistance with their lives.[3]

Among the writers from Equatorial Guinea, Bolekia is considered of the "lost generation," that is, those who had to leave their land due to internal oppression. Many of these poets, narrators, and political critics live in Spain today, wishing desperately for a change in regime that would allow them to return. In many ways the loss of a land, a culture, a childhood, a climate, a family network, old habits, and stories traveling from mouth to mouth, make up the primary sources for this poetry.[4]

But of course *Löbëla* (perhaps like the Bubi dictionary) is a work of resistance in an indirect way: by singing of his lost land, cavernous rocks, waters, plants, rituals, his gods and goddesses, damsels and gentlemen, gonads and vulvas, he utters a protest, a loud one. In the few prose sections of this collection he cries out poetically that he is recreating all of this because it is far removed from him (historically and politically). In a couple of instances he tells us he writes as an act of restoring his own memory, for to restore memory, in his case, is something like registering a protest. At the same time his desire to bring back the past, to bring back what has been taken from him, is something we can all share. And this is perhaps the most important feature of this collection for the English reader: that in virtually

---

3. See Bolekia's on historical account of Equatorial Guinea. *Aproximación a la historia de Guinea Ecuatorial*. Salamanca. Amarú. 2003.

4. The following texts, while by no means an exhaustive list, provide basic information in English on the history and contemporary petro-politics of Equatorial Guinea:
Max Liniger-Goumaz, *Historical Dictionary of Equatorial Guinea, Small is Not always Beautiful: The Story of Equatorial Guinea*; Peter Maas, "A Touch of Crude," *Mother Jones*, Jan/Feb., 2005; Ibrahim Sudiata, *Equatorial Guinea: colonialism, state terror, and the Search for Stability*; Ken Silverstein, "Oil Politics in the 'Kuwait of Africa," *The Nation*, April 22, 2002; Adam Roberts, *The Wonga Coup: Guns, Thugs, and a Ruthless Determination to Create Mayhem in an Oil-Rich Corner of Africa*; Robert Klitgaard, *Tropical Gangsters: One Man's Experience With Decadence and Development in Deepest Africa*.

Thoughts From the Translator

every poem in *Löbëla* one can hear a plea for the universal, as problematic as that term can be.

First, there is religion and spirituality. I find this collection filled with those two. While not the religious or spiritual tone and images we are used to, if we think about this tone and these images we'll see familiar transcendent themes. "Who is Löbëla?" the poet asks in his prose introduction to the second section of the collection (36), and the answer seems to be the question itself. Clearly if there is a religion alluded to in these verses it is not monotheistic; we find traces of paganism, animism, and worship of ancestors, a belief that the fallen members of the community will always be present. Indeed there is much in these poems about eternity and the continuation of life after death. I hear in these poems a manifestation of the Nietzschean dichotomy between the Babylonian and the Dionysian. Bolekia's gods and goddesses change names, genders, and identities. They participate in human endeavors, but at the same time they are objects of worship. And perhaps most importantly they come to life through their telling, that is, through stories and images created through the tradition of a community, in this case the oral tradition. Note for example (among many) the two poems in the section titled "The Goddess Löbëla" dealing with the history of the deity: "Löbëla" and "The Ballad of Löbëla." She "narrates her own destiny" (53) after the poet has described her in all her multifarious roles and characteristics: a Goddess-Mother, a lover, her long and sacred breasts, her androgyny–indeed in this poem as in others Löbëla creates herself: "sculpts her [own] desired limbs" (52). And in the following poem, the "Ballad of Löbëla" we read her legend. In this poem we sense the possibility of a creation myth. Löbëla is a wandering goddess who seems to float while her tears irrigate the land; her life-giving feature is perhaps her most important. But also crucial are her multiple identities, her many names. The wandering goddess poured blood on the palm tree and tinted her waters red (56), and she was possessed in order to "end the chaos" (57). Admittedly, this is all very mysterious; there is not a beginning, middle, and end to the ballad. What we have instead are images, segments of happenings that feel very much like a story of how it all began. But what makes this story stand out most vividly, in my reading, is its self-consciousness; the poet is laying bare that this is a story and he is the teller: "I will tell as long as someone listens/I tell the mysterious life of Löbëla and Wewèöpö [another deity fused with Löbëla]" (57). In this way–and in many other ways–the legend of Löbëla is universal: it comes to us through the telling.

Thoughts From the Translator

Moreover I find an ethical dimension to these poems. Not necessarily a conventional ethics of acceptable and non-acceptable behavior, but an ethics of the relationship between self and other. Many of these poems have to do with relationships, at times dialogues, at others interactions among a variety of characters. Note for example "Twenty and Ten" in the third section: a man and a woman (lovers? the beginning members of a family?) carve out a living for themselves in harmony, talking and listening, searching and finding, all in the context of building a hut (for "twenty and ten"), a dwelling for themselves and for the future. A more tender nuclear family one cannot conceive. And one of the few poems that cries out against open and cruel injustice of the political kind is "The Sentence," also in the third part of the collection. It is a poem in which we witness the execution and terror of who knows who. The last line incarnates Bolekia's sense of indignation: "the word liberty" (108) comes from the blood of ancestors, young men, and an entire "pueblo" (people, 108), a suggestion that the struggle will continue despite the loss (momentary) of life. We find all this ethical discourse in the context of an implicit (albeit clear, at least to me) statement that we are all one, made of language, as Bolekia says in the Epilogue, no matter if we are speakers of Bubi or Spanish or any specific language.

On the translation: a difficult task, I'm not sure if I have been "accurate." Difficult because, as the poet himself says, so much of the specificity of these verses relies on direct knowledge of Bubi beliefs and legends, to say nothing of the Bubi language. Yet I have tried to draw out the images of these beliefs and legends as I (one reader, a Spanish-English speaker) see, hear, taste, feel and understand them. I have tried to do justice to the poetry, because I firmly believe that when this poet tells us he is not a poet, he says so ironically: he is not a poet, "unless [or course] I search for the meaning of my journey through the language of my haphazard oppressor, an actor playing the role of someone engulfed in pain as I lay bare everything my ancestors were but I could not be" (Epilogue). And that is precisely what these verses do: "search for the meaning of a journey through language." Thus my role as translator is to highlight that poetry, to render (try to) in English that linguistic search.

One specific example among lots of them, is when, after much pondering, I grasped the image of Löbëla in the "rodetes" (58) ("rings," 56) of frost. Those "rodetes" were baffling to me; the word can have many meanings, but of course what I think Bolekia was looking for was a verbal picture of this mysterious goddess "walking" (while not stepping on land as he says) over the earth as if in mist: thus the rings of mist encircling her feet ("The Ballad of Löbëla") (56). In any case, as one who has written on, and who loves reciting aloud, the poetry of Lorca and Machado, I see images in Bolekia's verses much or something like those two archetypical Spanish poets, a likeness perhaps Bolekia would not be so sure of, but as a translator and a lover of poetry, I think that at times there is a resemblance. One example is that poem filled with moon images, "Waters and Moon" in which both appear as players in an incident recalled and related by the poet, like Lorca's "Moon Ballad."

In short: Justo Bolekia is a poet in spite of himself, and I hope you English-Spanish readers enjoy listening to him.

www.ingramcontent.com/pod-product-compliance
Lightning Source LLC
Chambersburg PA
CBHW050832160426
43192CB00010B/1998